African Arguments

Written by experts with an un~~~~~~ ~~~~~ ~~~~~~~~~,
African Arguments is a series of concise, engaging books that address
the key issues currently facing Africa. Topical and thought-provoking,
accessible but in-depth, they provide essential reading for anyone
interested in getting to the heart of both why contemporary Africa is
the way it is and how it is changing.

p. 157 kenya

African Arguments Online

African Arguments Online is a website managed by the Royal African
Society, which hosts debates on the African Arguments series and
other topical issues that affect Africa: http://africanarguments.org

Theodore Trefon, *Congo's Environmental Paradox: Potential and Predation in a Land of Plenty*

Paul Richards, *Ebola: How a People's Science Helped End an Epidemic*

Louisa Lombard, *State of Rebellion: Violence and Intervention in the Central African Republic*

Kris Berwouts, *Congo's Violent Peace: Conflict and Struggle Since the Great African War*

Hilary Matfess, *Women and the War on Boko Haram: Wives, Weapons, Witnesses*

Forthcoming titles

Mick Moore, Wilson Prichard, Odd-Helge Fjelstad, *Taxing Africa: Coercion, Reform and Development*

Ebenezer Obadare, *Pentecostal Republic: Religion and the Struggle for State Power in Nigeria*

Nanjala Nyabola, *Digital Democracy, Analogue Politics: How the Internet Era is Transforming Kenya*

Published by Zed Books and the IAI with the support of the following organisations:

The principal aim of the **International African Institute** is to promote scholarly understanding of Africa, notably its changing societies, cultures and languages. Founded in 1926 and based in London, it supports a range of publications including the journal *Africa*. www.internationalafricaninstitute.org

Now more than a hundred years old, the **Royal African Society** through its journal, *African Affairs*, and by organising meetings, discussions and other activities, strengthens links between Africa and Britain and encourages understanding of Africa and its relations with the rest of the world. www.royalafricansociety.org

The **World Peace Foundation**, founded in 1910, is located at the Fletcher School, Tufts University. The Foundation's mission is to promote innovative research and teaching, believing that these are critical to the challenges of making peace around the world, and should go hand in hand with advocacy and practical engagement with the toughest issues. www.worldpeacefoundation.org

About the author

Celeste Hicks is a freelance journalist who has been writing about Chad and the Sahel for more than ten years. Previously BBC correspondent in Chad and Mali, she worked for BBC World Service African Service in London before becoming an independent journalist in 2011. She writes for the BBC, the *Guardian*, *World Politics Review*, *Jane's Intelligence Review*, *Africa Report*, Bloomberg and many others. She is also the author of *Africa's New Oil* (Zed 2015).

THE TRIAL OF HISSÈNE HABRÉ

HOW THE PEOPLE OF CHAD BROUGHT A TYRANT TO JUSTICE

CELESTE HICKS

In association with
International African Institute
Royal African Society
World Peace Foundation

ZED

The Trial of Hissène Habré: How the People of Chad Brought a Tyrant to Justice
was first published in 2018 by Zed Books Ltd, The Foundry, 17 Oval Way, London
SE11 5RR, UK.

www.zedbooks.net

Typeset in Haarlemmer by seagulls.net
Index by John Barker
Cover design by Jonathan Pelham
Cover photo © Daniel Simon/Getty

A catalogue record for this book is available from the British Library

ISBN 978-1-78699-184-3 hb
ISBN 978-1-78699-183-6 pb
ISBN 978-1-78699-185-0 pdf
ISBN 978-1-78699-186-7 epub
ISBN 978-1-78699-187-4 mobi

Printed and bound by CPI Group (UK) Ltd, Croydon, CR0 4YY

CONTENTS

ACKNOWLEDGEMENTS

This book is dedicated to all the Chadian victims of Hissène Habré and the DDS for their tireless fight for justice.

With great thanks to Reed Brody, Henri Thulliez and Stephanie Hancock at Human Rights Watch for their ongoing support for the project and their invaluable institutional record of the twenty-five year fight for justice. Thanks to Miss Wasabi films, creators of the excellent film *Talking about Rose*, for the generous travel and writing grant which helped me to complete this project. Thanks also to Clement Abaifouta for helping me to access the Chadian victims in N'Djamena, to Jean Noyoma Kovousouma for his help and arrangements during my last visit, and to Jacqueline Moudeina for always agreeing to see me despite her general infuriation with journalists. Thanks to Mike Dottridge for his enthusiasm and attention to detail, filling in the many gaps about Habré's crimes in the 1980s, and to Kim Thuy Seelinger for tipping me off about the seminal importance of the Extraordinary African Chambers' work on sexual violence as a war crime. Thanks to Lucy Lamble at the *Guardian* for commissioning so many reports on this subject, and to Mark Kersten and Phil Clark for being great sounding boards and Matt Brown for his research assistance. Once again thanks to Ken Barlow at Zed Books and Stephanie Kitchen at the International African Institute for their faith in me, and to Dave for his clear thinking when I couldn't see the wood for the trees.

INTRODUCTION

For ninety days, Hissène Habré sat like a mannequin on a large black leather armchair at the front of the stuffy main courtroom of Dakar's Palais de Justice in Senegal. Every day he was dressed from head to foot in a gleaming white boubou (a long, flowing garment worn by men and women in parts of West Africa) presumably the miracle work of OMO washing powder and a dedicated cleaning lady hiding in the bowels of Cap Manuel prison where Habré had been incarcerated since 2013. The rough outline of his thin legs could be made out under the lines of the crisp boubou; never a large man, he was after all in his seventies when this trial began. He gripped a set of gris-gris beads in one hand, which was perched delicately on his lap. His head was wrapped in a pristine and perfectly folded white turban, with dark glasses resting on his petite turned up nose. Look a little closer and you could just make out the faint wrinkles on his forehead, a few grey hairs visible in his moustache. Apart from the odd moment where his crossed leg would twitch, he sat from morning to night for those three months barely flinching. Apart from on the first day of his trial, he never once spoke, asked for a glass of water, or took notes. Day in, day out, he stared ahead impassively, refusing to make eye contact with the judges, prosecutors and witnesses. It was easy to forget on some days that he was even there; an ethereal figure floating just off-centre of where all the action was taking place. He seemed somehow at odds with the drama of the stories being recounted to the court, tales of the gravest crimes imaginable: torture, war crimes, rape and crimes against humanity. Even when the guilty verdict was read out a year after the trial started, he showed little sign of emotion. The more I studied that image of the mannequin of Hissène Habré – in contrast to his better known persona as a much-feared dictator in 1980s Chad – the more I was drawn into the puzzle of his personality and this extraordinary story.

The evidence of the human rights abuses and violence which took place in Chad during the 1980s was overwhelming. Habré's government had been responsible for a network of secret prisons, night-time disappearances, the torture of political opponents, massacres and the destruction of entire villages. As head of state during that terrible time his ultimate responsibility for what happened was scarcely in doubt, but his trial in front of the specially created Extraordinary African Chambers (EAC) in 2015/16 unearthed many subtle and complex questions about bringing justice so long after the fact. Exactly how much had he known about the day-to-day practices of his secret police? Could he physically have personally directed everything or was much of the torture in fact carried out by his subordinates who never had to answer at this international trial? How much of his motivation was in the so-called 'national interest' in his battles with Colonel Muammar Qaddafi of Libya, and how much was it just to protect his own position? With his recalcitrant decision to remain silent and not to cooperate with the EAC tribunal, we will probably never know if he feels any regret for what happened, or remorse for all those who died. We will never know how he resisted the urge to defend himself during the months of gruelling testimony from almost a hundred victims and witnesses who testified. Was his silence an admission of guilt, or a brazen attempt to present himself as a martyr? Can former victims ever really move on without hearing the truth or without him asking their forgiveness? Is it enough to convict just one man who once sat at the top of a complex network of terror and surveillance involving hundreds of secret police and security agents? What about the role of France and the US, two world powers who did little to rein in the activities of Chad's secret police in the 1980s, despite significant international awareness of what was going on? These questions go right to the heart of the contemporary debates on the role of international justice for the victims of gross human rights abuses which have developed over the last twenty-five years.

Habré's story

Hissène Habré was president of Chad from 1982 to 1990, one of the most tumultuous periods in the country's remarkably turbulent history. During his rule, Chad was embroiled in a struggle for its very existence as Libyan troops under Colonel Qaddafi marched in and occupied a swathe of desert in the country's north. Supported by the US and France, Habré's FANT (National Armed Forces of Chad) led a protracted and bitter war against the occupying force from machine-gun-equipped Toyota land-cruisers, which eventually culminated in a humiliating defeat of the vastly better equipped Libyans at Ouadi Doum in 1987. During that time Habré also faced down round after round of domestic opposition from Goukouni Oueddei, the man he had toppled as president in 1982 and who was backed by Qaddafi, as well as rebellions in the south, north and east from several rival ethnic groups.

In order to focus on defeating Qaddafi, stabilise the country and consolidate his own position, Habré created a new national security agency, the DDS (Directorate of Documentation and Security), to crack down on domestic opposition. During the 1980s it is believed to have arrested, tortured and held in illegal detention tens of thousands of people, and killed or allowed the deaths of thousands. His victims have claimed that Habré ruled like a 'little God' and surrounded himself by associates and hangers on from his own Gorane (otherwise known as the Toubou or Teda) ethnic group. The methods employed in the DDS's network of secret prisons were truly horrifying, including hanging prisoners by their testicles, tying their hands and feet behind their backs, forcing them to drink water and tightening sticks around their skulls. Women and children were raped and hundreds succumbed to treatable diseases like dysentery and malaria, or died from malnourishment. Hundreds more disappeared without trace, and to this day relatives still do not know what happened to them. At the same time the police, army and security forces used brutal methods to suppress dissent in all corners of the country, including massacres of civilians and rebel fighters and torching and destroying entire villages. Prisoners of war (POWs) were kept in inhumane conditions for years without access to the Red Cross, and there were many alleged incidents of large numbers of former combatants being tied together and shot or even burnt to death. It has been alleged that the DDS had more than 40,000 victims.

When Habré was finally toppled by his former army chief Idriss Déby in 1990 following a brutal crackdown on Déby's own Zaghawa ethnic group, he disappeared into an obscure exile in Dakar, Senegal. For many years it looked as if the human rights abuses which took place in Chad during the 1980s would simply be forgotten; yet another unfortunate case of an African dictator committing crimes which no one ever realistically believed could be prosecuted. The only organisation able to gather evidence during the 1980s was Amnesty International, and its researchers today readily admit that in the 1980s and 1990s they had actually had little idea of the true scale of what had happened.[1] A 'Truth Commission' established in Chad in the early 1990s to gather evidence from Habré's victims once he had been forced from power rather boldly recommended he be prosecuted, but for many years Habré enjoyed de facto protection from various Senegalese administrations. Chad under Habré's successor Idriss Déby did not take any significant steps towards improving human rights and there was no realistic prospect of him being tried there. During those years, practices of international justice were still in their infancy and there had been criticisms that the international community had been slow to react to the horrors of the former Yugoslavia, Rwanda, Sierra Leone and Liberia.

However Habré's crimes would not be forgotten by everyone, and in the early 1990s a group of former prisoners of the DDS jails began to organise and collect testimony of their experiences, helped by a small number of dedicated Chadian lawyers. In 2000, supported by the international organisation Human Rights Watch (HRW), they launched an audacious attempt at seeking justice, which led to Habré being indicted in Senegal for human rights crimes. However, due to political pressure at the highest levels in Senegal, these early successes did not bear fruit and Habré enjoyed another twelve years in exile without fear of prosecution. Several ingenious attempts to bring him to justice involving Belgium and the West African regional body ECOWAS (Economic Community of West African States) failed or became hamstrung by seemingly terminal delays. By 2011 it seemed to be almost impossible to imagine the former president ever being brought before a court.

Nevertheless, the very next year there was a remarkable turnaround, demonstrating the strong link between justice and politics. In April 2012 Abdoulaye Wade, who had for many years resisted attempts to move forward with a prosecution of Habré, was replaced by Macky Sall as the new Senegalese president. With his cooperation and a stinging rebuke to Senegal from the International Court of Justice for its failure to prosecute the former Chadian president, things began to move very fast. In 2013 the African Union (AU) set up an entirely new international judicial entity, the EAC, and indicted Habré and five co-accused DDS agents for war crimes, crimes against humanity and torture committed in Chad from 1982 to 1990. After a ground-breaking pre-trial investigation phase which involved four research commissions to Chad where prosecutors heard from hundreds of witnesses and excavated mass graves, on 20 July 2015 that trial finally got underway. On the first day Hissène Habré was literally dragged kicking and screaming into court in the Palais de Justice in Dakar and was held down by masked Senegalese security agents. After a histrionic performance in which he denounced the court as an imperialist institution, the trial got down to serious business in September 2015, and interviewed some ninety witnesses and victims. This was the first time the courts of one African country had been used to try a former leader of another African country and the judge's bench was entirely made up of African judges and prosecutors. It was also the first time a universal jurisdiction case (which gives states the power to prosecute crimes which took place in other countries) had progressed to trial in Africa.

The establishment of the EAC is a remarkable story of how grassroots justice played a vital role in the building of a prosecution of a former African strongman. This book is dedicated to the tireless efforts of the Chadian victims' associations, activists, human rights campaigners and lawyers who refused ever to give up in the face of almost overwhelming pessimism that their quest for justice would succeed.

However, the trial before the EAC in Senegal does not only bear significance for the victims of Habré's abuses and the shape of domestic politics and justice in Chad. It has wide and mostly under-explored implications for other forms of international justice being employed around the world today. It did not happen in a void. As Africa's relationship with the International Criminal Court (ICC) has become increasingly problematic in recent years, there is now a renewed interest in other forms of trial and what they can do to deliver timely justice for victims of abuses.

Africa and the ICC

The ICC is based in The Hague with the power to try genocide, crimes against humanity and war crimes. The Rome Statute which established it made a firm commitment to end impunity. The document was drawn up at a time when international justice was learning fast lessons from the experience of establishing tribunals to prosecute the crimes against humanity committed in the former Yugoslavia (International Criminal Tribunal for the former Yugo-

slavia, ICTY) and the genocide in Rwanda (International Cr_____
Tribunal for Rwanda, ICTR). The Rome Statute aimed to build on
concepts such as fundamental human rights, which had emerged
in the aftermath of the Second World War and been enshrined
in the UN Declaration of Human Rights in 1948. However, these
ideas had remained somewhat theoretical and there was little international will to deal with domestic crimes committed by despotic
leaders who had been 'on the right side of history'. As Tim Allen
argues, 'Leaders like ... Mengistu, Pinochet, Mobutu and Barre
acted without any expectation that they would ever be prosecuted
for their barbaric behaviour'.[2]

When the ICC was formally launched in 2002, there was much
interest in Africa. Several African countries had been involved
in the discussions to set up the court, keen to find a way to put
an end to human rights abuses and violence which at times had
seemed to plague the continent. Many human rights groups were
pleased at the prospect of a permanent body dedicated to bringing
prosecutions for international crimes, with a global machinery
in place and ready to investigate and prosecute crimes perhaps
even as they happened. Thirty-four African countries were early
signatories and the first ICC referrals were from Uganda, asking
for help investigating human rights abuses being committed by
the Lord's Resistance Army (LRA) in the country's north, and
then from the Democratic Republic of Congo (DRC) to investigate the situation in the country's restive eastern provinces. Both
these cases were taken up by the court's first chief prosecutor, Luis
Moreno-Ocampo.

However, it did not take long for the relationship with Africa
to deteriorate. The first real signs of trouble came when the ICC
indicted the sitting Sudanese President Omar Al-Bashir for crimes
committed in the Darfur region of Sudan. The decision put the
court on a collision course with the AU, which had initially been
supportive of the court, because of the perceived threat to the
principle of immunity for a sitting head of state, which has been a

central tenet of the political leadership of the body. It also caused a vitriolic campaign of rejection from within Sudan with many arguing the arrest warrant against Al-Bashir was hindering the prospects of bringing peace in Darfur. At the same time Uganda's President Yoweri Museveni seemed to rethink his earlier enthusiasm for the court, and the arrest warrants issued against leaders of the LRA rebel movement began to be seen as obstacles to peace talks in some quarters. Things really got tricky when the ICC decided in 2010 to indict six Kenyans for their role in post-electoral violence in late 2007 in which an estimated 1200 people had died. When two of those individuals – Uhuru Kenyatta and William Ruto – were elected President and Vice President of Kenya in 2013, the ICC was faced with an unprecedented diplomatic crisis. Added to these criticisms was the fact that, to date, all of the cases at the ICC which have proceeded to trial have involved Africans. While many grassroots justice organisations and victims' groups across Africa, and indeed several African leaders, remain strongly supportive of the institution and have continued to engage, there has also been a sustained attack by other African leaders. It has been criticised for being anti-African, and in more extreme opinions has been called racist. It has been accused of only being effective in the prosecution of 'small fry', with many of its prosecutions being for relatively minor figures such as rebel leaders in regional conflicts. This push-back against the institution led to three nations – Burundi, the Gambia and South Africa – signalling their intention to withdraw from the Rome Statute in 2016, and the AU issuing a non-binding statement calling on African nations to withdraw from the ICC at its summit in early 2017.

While the Habré case could never have been prosecuted by the ICC, as his crimes were committed before the Rome Statute came into effect in 2002, the EAC's success in prosecuting and convicting a former African head of state for crimes committed on his watch has been observed with interest by many sections of the human rights community in Africa. As the scale of the problems faced by the ICC has become evident, this book aims to examine how alternative forms of justice could now be further developed. Although there are of course alternative approaches to responding to human rights abuses that do not involve criminal prosecutions, this book will mostly focus on the aspects of the EAC and hybrid trials that might be replicated, and what role these might play in the future of prosecutions of human rights abuses in Africa and beyond.

The Habré case: the rebirth of the hybrid court?

The EAC was an example of a hybrid court, which means a court that employs both international and domestic law, and international and domestic personnel. Hybrid courts, which are normally designed to investigate and prosecute one individual case or situation, became popular in the late 1990s and early 2000s in the so-called 'interregnum period' between the establishment of the permanent ICC in 1998 and the coming into force of its statute in 2002. They are sometimes referred to as the 'third generation' of criminal courts – the Nuremberg model being the first and purely international 'ad hoc' bodies such as the ICTY and the ICTR being the second. The first such court was the Special Court for Sierra Leone (SCSL) which was established in 2002, followed by the Extraordinary Chambers in the Courts of Cambodia (ECCC). Hybrids were seen as a 'natural evolution of international criminal justice' and promised an alternative to domestic prosecutions, which were often politically impossible, without having to turn to big international trials such as the ICTY and the ICTR. However hybrid trials also began to be criticised for not being strong enough to withstand domestic political pressures – for example the Cambodian trial struggled to deal with the legacy of the Khmer Rouge in Cambodian society – and for not doing enough to influence the capacities of domestic justice systems. In the early 2000s as the ICC prepared to open its doors, much debate on international justice assumed that hybrid trials would cease to be relevant as the ICC would effectively remove the need for them.

However, as we will see, the ICC's path has not been as smooth as expected, and the success of the EAC case has shown how the hybrid model may now start to come back into fashion. 'The ICC was meant to replace hybrid tribunals but the reality has been much messier than that',[3] says legal author and academic Phil Clark. The EAC case had a number of positives. Where hybrid tribunals may in the past have seemed to have a limited and in some cases even negligible impact on domestic justice and commitments to inform the public, the EAC in fact was notable for the presence of several prominent Chadian lawyers acting on behalf of the civil parties set up to represent the victims, who were a vital and vocal part of the trial. It also had a credit-worthy outreach programme which started before the trial began and is still running today. In striking contrast to the ICC's perceived anti-African bias, the EAC bench and prosecuting team was made up entirely of Africans, and the court was held in Senegal – though obviously not in Chad itself it was nevertheless much closer to the communities affected by the crimes than The Hague. 'It has shown us what future regional hybrid tribunals, or even so-called 'pop-up' courts might look like', says Kim Thuy Seelinger, Director of the Sexual Violence Program at the Human Rights Center, University of California Berkeley, School of Law.[4] It was also meticulous in its strict adherence to schedule and its small budget. The trial phase ran for just under one year, with all the witnesses being heard in three months. The court never had to ask for additional funding beyond its original allocation of €8.6 million ($10.32 million), a notable achievement, which offers the prospect of relatively cheap, quick trials being put together in the future.

Already two new hybrid trials are being proposed in Africa, to deal with human rights abuses in the Central African Republic (CAR) and also South Sudan. Considering that for many activists and observers the ICC's difficulties represent a serious challenge to the future of international justice, this book will attempt to highlight the key strengths and weaknesses of the EAC and ask whether significant elements of it can be reproduced in future hybrid trials.

Could the 'next generation' look something like a 'quick response' ad hoc hybrid court with a team of roving African judges and personnel which could be rapidly deployed in the aftermath of civil conflicts? Can Senegal now build on its reputation for successfully handling an international case and start trying other international cases? With regard to the ICC, which has a poor record in prosecuting the highest level officials while still in office, the book explores whether the EAC model could do better at bringing former dictators to justice once they have left power. Importantly the book analyses the question of whether the EAC only came about because of a unique confluence of events which, practically, will never happen again.

 Chapter 1 looks at the historical background and extraordinary power politics of early 1980s Chad, as Hissène Habré seized power in the most Machiavellian way and went on to turn all the organs of state security to his advantage. It examines the high-stakes battle against the Libyan occupation of the Aouzou strip, a narrow band of desert north of Faya Largeau. It looks at how the US and to a lesser extent France seemed willing to tolerate and to some extent support Habré's brutal suppression of his own people simply because he was viewed as a useful proxy in the Cold War battle against Colonel Qaddafi. Chapter 2 considers Habré's prolonged and comfortable stay in Senegal during the 1990s and 2000s, examining the role played by Senegal's former President Abdoulaye Wade in shielding his 'brother from the African heads of state trade union' from prosecution. It traces the growing grassroots justice movement forming in Chad from the early 1990s which pushed for a prosecution under the guidance of international human rights organisations, and details the three failed attempts to prosecute the former president before the EAC was finally set up by the AU in 2013.

Chapter 3 charts the dramatic course of the trial itself in Senegal in 2015/16. Powerful and shocking testimony emerged from the ninety-day witness phase, including extraordinary claims that Habré himself had raped one of the victims. The former president confounded everyone by refusing point blank to cooperate with the court or even the defence lawyers who had been appointed by the court on his behalf to ensure a fair trial. It examines the strength of the verdict, the appeal against his conviction which was finally rejected in April 2017 (and bizarrely launched without Habré's approval) and the so far fruitless attempts to compensate his victims. Chapter 4 looks at the impact of the EAC on Chad and Chadians. It examines in detail the EAC's impressive outreach programme in Chad itself, and asks to what extent the court has been able to restore local faith in justice. We learn how the determined victims have responded to the trial, and whether they have since been able to move on with their lives. We also hear from ordinary Chadians about their views on the trial, and examine what impacts the EAC has had on domestic justice and justice systems in Senegal. Chapter 5 contextualises the EAC on a timeline of developing international justice, from the ad hoc trials of the 1990s, through the establishment of the hybrids and the ICC which was expected to replace everything. It examines what has gone wrong in Africa's relationship with the ICC and asks what role the hybrid trial will play in future. It also makes practical suggestions of features and aspects of the EAC which may be of use in future justice projects.

The research for this book has been carried out intermittently over the ten years I have been writing about Chad, the wider Sahel and West and North Africa. I lived and worked in Chad as BBC correspondent from 2008 to 2010 and since then have returned on many occasions to follow up long-term research ideas as a freelance journalist. My first book, which included an in-depth analysis of Chad's poorly managed oil project, was published in 2015. Despite vowing that I would wait a few years before even contemplating writing another book, the drama of Habré's story proved too tempting. Before 2011, I carried out many interviews with the key players such as Jacqueline Moudeina and Clement Abaifouta as the attempts to bring Habré to justice twisted and turned. I confess to having been one of the many pessimistic voices proclaiming that it seemed unlikely that the former president would ever be brought to justice. However, as the momentum for the EAC built from 2012 onwards and confidence grew that he would indeed be tried in Dakar, I felt more and more compelled to write the full story. My early research was greatly augmented through two working visits to Dakar during the EAC trial phase in 2015/16, and was followed up by at least fifty face-to-face, phone or Skype interviews with key players since the verdict was announced in May 2016. In January 2017 I completed a further research trip to N'Djamena to carry out a number of interviews focusing on the longer-term impact of the Habré story on both victims and ordinary Chadians. For the aspects of the book which concern the as yet largely unexplored question of the EAC's place in the development of international justice, I have relied heavily on my experience working on the daily news grind at BBC World Service Africa from 2005 to 2014, where I reported regularly on the difficulties faced by the ICC and its relationship with Africa. I have also consulted widely among current writers and thinkers on international justice and I am eternally grateful for the help of a small band of dedicated Habré-watchers for their support.

What follows is simply a remarkable tale of one man's brutal attempts to hang on to power in a period of intense political turmoil set against the dramatic backdrop of the 1980s and the Cold War. This is followed by the incredible story of how the victims of this shocking cruelty carried on in the face of almost universal pessimism, and at times ridicule, to ensure that a tyrant was eventually brought to justice.

was he?

Chapter 1

FROM THE PRESIDENTIAL PALACE TO OUAKAM

Habré's route to power

Independence was never going to be easy for Chad. Of little use to France during its colonial occupation of Central and West Africa, it had been incorporated into French Equatorial Africa in 1920. The entire northern half of the country, mostly rocky Saharan desert, had been classified as 'Tchad Inutile' (Useless Chad), and development, in particular raising educational levels, had been concentrated in the 'utile' and more fertile south. Chad lagged behind other African colonies such as Senegal or Côte d'Ivoire. There was no railway, hardly any roads, and it was seen primarily as a source of raw materials including cotton. Politically it was as unstable as a country could be, and when it gained independence in August 1960 along with most of the other former French colonies, there was barely a government to speak of. Political parties did exist but they were factional, badly organised and poorly funded; there were strong ethnic rivalries between the mostly Muslim and pastoralist north and the mostly Christian southern sedentary farmers.

Into this breach stepped François Tombalbaye, a Sara from Chad's more fertile southern Sahel belt who had received a French education. He was the leader of the PPT (Chadian Progressive Party), which had led Chad's largely tokenistic government under French rule. Although he assumed power in 1960 without any obvious rival, it didn't take him long to begin to alienate Chad's political class.[1] From the early days of his rule, his tendency to promote and concentrate power in the hands of southerners exacerbated those regional geographical and ethnic tensions which had existed during French rule. Democracy got off to a poor start. Just two years after independence in 1962, he took the major step of dissolving all political parties except the PPT, and followed it with the National Assembly just a few days later.

Tombalbaye's seeming dependence on France was a source of resentment and tension, though his policy vis-à-vis the former colonial power was never consistent. Although France had formally decolonised, in practice it retained a large presence in Chad which was mostly occupied with securing cheap Chadian cotton for French mills. This all came to a head in 1964 when Tombalbaye suddenly ordered the former colonial power to reduce its military presence in the BET province (Borkou Ennedi Tibesti) – Chad's vast desert north. Suddenly the bulk of competent former colonial officials were pushed aside in favour of less skilled southerners. Along with his policy of 'Africanisation' which involved replacing French names and places with traditional African ones, this created resentment among the northerners who felt the southern officials had little understanding of life in the desert. In protest, the first of an almost interminable list of Chadian desert revolts began in the early 1960s in Bardai, in the Teda/Daza heartlands of the desert, and soon spread to nearby Zouar.[2] Popular discontent spread to other parts of the country. In November 1965 a rise in local taxes prompted people in the central town of Mangalmé to take to the streets; a visit by the country's Interior Minister in a bid to quell the protests led to riots in the streets in which an estimated 500 people were killed by security forces, one of the worst massacres in Chad's history.

The various rebellions which began to break out on a number of fronts from Guera to Wadai to Lake Chad during the 1960s and early 1970s proved extremely problematic for Tombalbaye and his largely ineffective army. Eventually some of these forces came together and coalesced into a new rebel group, the Chad National Liberation Front (FROLINAT), which was founded at Nyala in Darfur in June 1966. FROLINAT would go on to dominate Chadian politics for years to come. Initially led by the dissident Ibrahim Abatcha, the group expanded rapidly, bringing in other discontents from northern and eastern groups such as the Zaghawa, Massalit and Toubou. Over the next few years there followed repeated clashes between the government and the rebels and eastern Chad began to slip out of central government's control. As the revolt grew, Tombalbaye was only able to hold on by the skin of his teeth after being forced to appeal to the French for military assistance, which was reluctantly provided. In return for French military support, he begrudgingly agreed to a programme of moderate political and tax reforms which briefly calmed tensions. In 1969 he won another term as president, but he had been the only candidate on the ballot.

Nevertheless, this brief respite in Chad's political chaos was not to last. Trouble was brewing on the northern border. In 1969 a group of army officers led by the then unknown Colonel Muammar Qaddafi had overthrown King Idris in Libya. Almost immediately, Qaddafi's unpredictable and expansionist pan-Arab agenda began to emerge and he took an interest in Chad and in stoking the rebellions. The first permanent base of FROLINAT was opened in Tripoli in 1969 and Qaddafi hosted a number of the Toubou leaders. To many observers' surprise, he also revived Libya's territorial claim to the Aouzou strip, a 43,000-square-mile piece of desert situated in northern Chad and containing a small oasis. This territory had been granted to Benito Mussolini's Italian colonial presence in Libya by representatives of the French colonial government in 1935, but this treaty was never ratified by France, and during the chaos of the Second World War it appeared to have been forgotten about. But not by Qaddafi. Not long after he came to power, his cartographers issued new maps showing that the border between Libya and Chad had been moved south by approximately sixty miles. In 1971 Tombalbaye narrowly escaped a coup plot which many suspected had been backed by Libya, and in 1972, during FROLINAT incursions into the BET, clear evidence of Libyan weaponry and support was found among the rebels. But Libya's ambitions were much larger than that, and in 1973, just six months after Chad and Libya had signed a harmless-looking Treaty of Friendship, Libyan soldiers moved into the Aouzou strip on the basis of the 1935 agreement. Tombalbaye was furious but largely powerless to act. His only recourse was to submit a complaint to the Organisation of African Unity (OAU), which was opposed to interference with colonial boundaries.

Into this cross-border postcolonial mess stepped Hissène Habré, the illegitimate son of a herder born in Faya Largeau in 1942, the same year as Colonel Qaddafi. He is a Toubou (Gorane is the Arabic name and the group is also known as the Teda) from the Anakaza sub-sub-clan of the Daza, a plain-dwelling non-aristocratic branch of the largely nomadic Toubou, a heritage which has pitted him against the group's higher-status traditional leaders throughout his life. After a primary school education, he became a sub-prefect in Faya Largeau. His intelligence was soon noticed by French officials in Chad's BET province, and he was chosen to attend the Institut de Droit Publique in Paris and then went on to study at the Institute des Sciences Politiques, where he stood out as an excellent student.[3] On his return to Chad in 1971, and still in his early twenties, he had seemed so impressive that it was said that Tombalbaye had personally asked him to return to carry out a secret mission to Libya.[4] But it wasn't long before he showed his true colours and made contact with the leaders of FROLINAT. Quickly he was appointed by the 'Derde', the non-hereditary elected leader of the Toubou, to lead the FROLINAT Second Army. This choice was to set him on a path of ineluctable rivalry with the son of the Derde, Goukouni Oueddei, another prominent commander of FROLINAT forces, which would last for the next fifteen years.

Hissène Habré first came to international attention in 1974 when his fighters attacked the desert oasis of Bardai and took hostage three young Europeans who were working on an archaeology project in the caves and oases of the Sahara. The French media lapped up the audacious demands for a ransom and the plight of the young archaeologist Françoise Claustre, whose husband was also kidnapped when he rushed to Tibesti to help her. A French intermediary, Captain Pierre Galopin, was executed by the rebels when he was sent to negotiate the hostages' release. Habré soon realised the value of his captives, and demanded a higher ransom and weapons for his cause. The hostages created a delicate and protracted political crisis with France which was to last until they were finally released in 1977.

The end of Tombalbaye

By 1975 the writing was on the wall for President François Tombalbaye, who had by then changed his name to Ngarta (chief) Tombalbaye as part of his 'authenticity' Africanisation drive. He continued to anger the northerners by his brutal suppression of the FROLINAT revolt and the imposition of what was perceived to be a southern initiation ceremony for any recruits to government positions. The French had become tired of his refusal to usher in political reforms and his seemingly schizophrenic dalliances with Qaddafi. In the end, drought in the Sahel, economic crisis and the failure to pay salaries all coalesced into a wave of domestic discontent with his rule. When he began to crack down on dissent by arresting a number of officers in the army, including the popular General Felix Malloum, it was only a matter of time before a military coup was launched. On 12 April 1975 rebel soldiers broke into the presidential palace on the banks of the Chari River in central N'Djamena and Tombalbaye was killed. Malloum, the former commander in chief of Chad's armed forces, became Chad's new president.[5]

However, Malloum fared little better than Tombalbaye in resolving the innate tensions in a land of marked geographical and demographic contrasts, where poverty, lack of development and tribal rivalries continued to challenge the ability of central government to control remote hinterlands. Libya's Colonel Qaddafi had no time for him. In August 1975 Libya formally annexed the Aouzou strip and as the situation deteriorated, Malloum was forced against his better judgement to turn to France for help. France, which was still in the afterglow of Charles De Gaulle's commitment to the former African colonies, responded favourably and dispatched a contingent of soldiers to protect Chad's territorial integrity. Once tensions were calmed, talks began; and in 1978, under pressure from Sudan, which was concerned about Chadian rebel activities in its western Darfur region, Malloum seemingly foolishly agreed to allow the ruthlessly ambitious Hissène Habré to become Prime Minister.

Again this political arrangement was not to last, and by 1979 Habré's loyalties were exposed – fighting broke out between his forces, the FAN (Armed Forces of the North), and Malloum's national army in the streets of N'Djamena. Goukouni Oueddei, the great Toubou rival who had opposed Habré's decision to serve under Malloum, and enjoyed the support of Libya, saw his opportunity to attack. He led his newly formed FAP (Popular Armed Forces), the remnants of FROLINAT, into battle with Habré's FAN forces. N'Djamena was brought to its knees by a bloody and confusing three-way battle. As the skirmishes continued, this chaos of shifting alliances gradually eroded the authority of Malloum and Chad's national transitional government. At a peace conference in 1979 in Kano, Nigeria, Malloum was forced into exile. Finally Goukouni Oueddei emerged as president of a newly formed Transitional National Government of Chad (GUNT), with Habré as Minister of Defence and members of FROLINAT in most key positions.

But the rivalry between Goukouni and Habré could also not be contained. Less than a year later, in early 1980, bitter fighting between Habré's FAN and Goukouni's FAP broke out on the streets of N'Djamena. In a brutal wave of killings and displacement, at least 3000 people are thought to have been killed. Thousands fled as refugees into neighbouring countries as the rival militias clashed, and N'Djamena was heavily damaged. The carnage only ended when Qaddafi sent 4000 troops from Aouzou to help President Goukouni – which was viewed as a deep humiliation and betrayal by many Chadians. Unable to stand up to the Libyans, Habré was forced into exile in Cameroon in late 1980.

But he was far from finished. From exile, he planned his revenge. Always a staunch opponent of Libya, his resolve was hardened by Qaddafi's announcement in January 1981 that Libya and Chad under Goukouni and his GUNT were now unified as one country. This news also worried regional leaders, who proposed the organisation of an African peacekeeping mission under the auspices of the OAU, which was intended to replace Libyan troops. However, at the end of 1981, perhaps sensing how unpopular Qaddafi was in Chad, Goukouni Oueddei's GUNT surprisingly ordered the Libyan troops to leave. Even more surprisingly they did, leaving Chad dangerously exposed to Habré's forces which had been rearming and reorganising in Darfur. In December 1981 the first ever African peacekeeping mission, 3000 strong, finally deployed to Chad. But it was already too late. By the end of the year, Habré's FAN had attacked and occupied Adré, Guereda, Iriba and, significantly, Abeche. He began a deadly march westwards, straight towards N'Djamena, with the OAU force looking on helplessly.[6] On 7 June 1982 Habré marched with his troops victoriously into the capital. Goukouni reportedly stormed out of an OAU meeting convened to solve the political crisis, shouting 'I am betrayed!' He disappeared into exile in Cameroon.

Habré in power

Hissène Habré's eight-year rule is remembered by many Chadians as the country's darkest time. Evidence of Habré's brutality already existed in the form of a number of mass graves which had been discovered near his home in N'Djamena following his retreat from the capital after the deadly FAN–FAP clashes of 1980.[7] His determination to acquire power and eliminate his rivals had been proven beyond all doubt. The country's chronic instability had been exposed and there was a continuing threat of violence and rebellion, with Libya snapping at his heels. In order to assert control, almost as soon as he was settled into N'Djamena's Presidential Palace Habré established a single ruling party, the UNIR (National Union for Independence and Revolution) which he controlled with an iron grip. He established the military's power through the National Armed Forces Command Council (CCFAN), which was almost completely dominated by his Gorane kinsmen (another name for the Toubou) from northern Chad. Half the country's national budget was dedicated to the military. He set about forming 'a dictatorship without precedent and attempted to destroy all forms of opposition'.[8]

Before long Habré had put in place a complex new system of information and security reporting, which included the DDS, a new agency which was dedicated to spying and reporting on all behaviour and activity of ordinary Chadians suspected of being against 'the national interest'. According to one report uncovered by HRW,[9] the DDS constituted 'the eyes and ears of the President of the Republic' and reported to him on a daily basis, although as we shall see, the extent to which Habré was directly responsible for the acts of torture carried out by his operatives in his name was to become hotly disputed during the court case against him in 2015–16. Originally designed to collect information to be used in the fight against Libya, the DDS soon became charged with gathering even the smallest details about any political opposition. It worked on a system of information sharing and denouncement which could easily land friends, colleagues and even family members in jail. All members of the DDS were obliged to swear an oath of loyalty to the president when they took up their jobs. The agency had tentacles right across the country, including a branch in every electoral borough. It was rapidly expanded in the early

1980s to include a number of new services such as the Presidential Investigation Service and the armed wing, the Special Rapid
Action Brigade (BSIR), which carried out arrests, tortures and
executions. These intelligence services, the army and secret police,
contributed to an overwhelming system of surveillance and punishment, which created a climate of fear in Chad in the 1980s. All four
directors of the DDS during the 1980s – Salah Younouss, Guihini
Korei, Ahmat Allatchi and Toke Dadi – were from Habré's Gorane
ethnic group.

Political prisoners were held in a network of jails where the DDS
came directly to carry out interrogations, and information about all
detainees was held at DDS headquarters. Proper judicial process for
those brought in for questioning was often ignored. Many of these
prisons were secret. The most notorious was known as 'La Piscine',
an underground interrogation centre in a former indoor swimming
pool used by families of colonial officers during French rule. Cells
in La Piscine were no bigger than 3 metres square, and would often
contain up to fifty prisoners. Being underground it became stifling
in the hot summer months when temperatures regularly reach over
45°C. In N'Djamena there were six other prisons – 'Les Locaux'
in a former French colonial commissariat building, the Camp
des Martyrs on a military base, the Gendarmerie camp, a prison
in the grounds of the presidential palace next to one of Habré's
offices which welcomed 'special prisoners' including members of
Goukouni Oueddei's family, the BSIR prison and the prison de
Moursal, which was created towards the end of Habré's rule. Conditions in all these prisons were described as appalling, with flooding,
infestations, little ventilation and massive overcrowding.[10]

The methods used in these prisons were recounted in horrifying
detail during the trial of Habré which took place in Senegal in 2015,
and were also collected in a Commission of Enquiry – including
drawings – published by the Chadian government in 1993. They
included punishments such as tying a prisoner's hands and feet
behind his back in a crippling position known as *arbatachar* ('14'

in Arabic), forcing water down prisoners' throats with a funnel, hanging prisoners by the testicles, spraying insecticide in the eyes, pulling out finger and toe nails, tightening sticks around the skull (known as the 'baguettes') and inserting the exhaust pipe of a running car engine in prisoners' mouths. Hundreds of people died in these jails, with reports of deaths almost every day. If not from the torture and injury, they succumbed to chronic overcrowding, neglect, poor diet, lack of water in stifling heat, unsanitary conditions, disease and infection caused by leaving dead bodies locked in airless cells with living prisoners. Survivors lost brain function due to sustained periods of eating poor quality food; inmates were forced to collect and remove the faeces of fellow inmates who could no longer walk. The ultimate humiliation came as surviving prisoners were forced to dig the graves of those who had died in detention, usually at Hamral-Goz, 'the Plain of the Dead', some ten kilometres from N'Djamena.[11]

Marguerite Garling, a researcher for Amnesty International's Africa programme, met exiles from the Habré regime who had fled to Paris in the 1980s, many of whom had been tortured and spent time in these prisons. It was a life-changing experience for her. 'We realised that some of those who came to tell us their stories became emotionally dependent on us. They often had no-one else to talk to. In the 1980s we were really working in a vacuum. We simply didn't realise the sheer dimension of what had been going on until after Habré had been deposed.'[12]

In addition to the detentions and disappearances in the capital, Habré's rule also saw a number of campaigns against ethnic groups in other parts of the country who rebelled against his presidency. His FAN armed forces had already come into conflict with elements of the FAT (Armed Forces of Chad) loyal to Wadel Abdelkader Kamougue, a southerner and former commander of the armed forces, in the late 1970s and early 1980s. Kamougue had begun to establish his own anti-Habré power base in the Christian-majority south. Once in power Habré had stepped up his policy of forcibly pacifying the south, sending in his newly formed FANT. During this repression, some Muslim units of the FANT had terrorised the southern population, leading to the emergence of a group known as 'Codos', an armed anti-Habré coalition. Beginning with what became known as 'Black September' in 1984, the president launched a sustained period of repression against the Codos commandos and the civilian population – intellectuals and military leaders were arbitrarily arrested and villages targeted for having collaborated with the rebels. Later in his presidency, Habré turned his bile on the Arab Chadian, Hadjerai and Zaghawa communities, which had hitherto been his northern allies, after a series of plots and threats to his rule were uncovered. These policies of ethnic oppression were often carried out by the DDS. Habré's security apparatus was also responsible for the deaths of numerous enemy combatants, with HRW documenting cases of large groups of GUNT soldiers and Libyan prisoners of war being arrested and executed, or simply disappearing.[13]

Exceptional times, exceptional measures?

This reign of oppression took place during a period of exceptional instability and existential crisis for Chad. Libya's aggression and invasion of the north could not be ignored. Habré kept in limitless supply his vitriol against Qaddafi and his policy of expansion, and vowed to rid Chad of the Libyan invaders. The war against Libya and the battle against Libyan-backed rebels would dominate his presidency and was from the beginning an uphill task. Almost as soon as Goukouni Oueddei had been forced from power in 1982, he had vowed to retake power with Libyan arms and support. His counter-attack against Habré was swift and effective. The first serious setback came in June 1983 when Goukouni's GUNT forces, backed by Libyan troops and air power, attacked and briefly held Habré's home town Faya Largeau in the north, and the important urban centre of Abeche in the east. In the following weeks, rebel forces went on to take several towns in the north and centre of Chad including Fada, Ouniango-Kebir and Zouar. By August the GUNT had advanced as far as just 300 kilometres north of N'Djamena. The world was forced to sit up and take notice. Habré was so worried that he travelled to the north to personally command the FANT in battle.

Despite deep political misgivings and reluctance, the same month France approved deployment of around 2700 troops and eight fighter jets to Chad to protect Habré's government. It would become known as Operation Manta. However Manta was never conceived as a method to reclaim territory for the Chadians, and what followed was a tacit acceptance of what was known as the 'politics of the 16th parallel'.[14] Although Habré succeeded in reclaiming Faya Largeau, Chad was de facto split in two following the Libyan/GUNT advance, with the Libyans/GUNT controlling the BET north of the 16th parallel line, which stretched roughly from the northern part of Kanem in the west to Oum Chalouba in the east, and France and Habré's forces holding the south. As long as the Libyan-backed GUNT refrained from crossing this red line, French President François Mitterrand was insistent that Manta would not directly challenge Qaddafi.

It was a poor compromise, but allowed a period of relative calm for the next three years. Skirmishes and internecine squabbles between GUNT factions continued, and a series of largely moribund peace conferences were unable to pacify Chad or conclusively deal with the Libyan invasion, which Habré was resolved not to tolerate. It was not until early 1986 that Oueddei's GUNT, backed by Libyan troops and air power, was able to regroup sufficiently to launch another attack over the 16th parallel. This time they got close to threatening Abeche and N'Djamena airport was bombed by Libyan planes, although eventually Habré's FAN was able to strike back and reclaim lost territory. The attack sparked France to launch a new deployment of 1000 troops to Chad, known as Operation Épervier (Sparrowhawk), which was to remain in Chad until 2014.

By the beginning of 1987, the Libyan presence in the BET was at least 5000 soldiers strong, backed up with the arrival of several thousand more specially trained Islamic Legionnaires, Mi24 helicopters and combat aircraft. However, it was the never-ending squabbles between Qaddafi's Chadian allies that would set the scene for the final stages of what became dubbed the 'Toyota Wars' – referring to the heavily armed pick-up trucks mounted with machine guns with which Habré and Goukouni's forces waged war (and a dominant feature to this day of rebellions in eastern Chad). Qaddafi had become increasingly disillusioned with Goukouni, who despite several years' worth of Libyan arms and supplies had been unable to overthrow Habré. In late 1986 Qaddafi reorganised the GUNT leadership and the humiliated Goukouni was demoted and eventually landed up in jail in Tripoli. But in reality Qaddafi had no one else he could trust among the motley collection of Chadian rebels scattered across the north and east of the country. The rebels refused to unite under Wadel Kamougue, or under the mercurial Achiekh Ibn-Oumar, who led another FROLINAT splinter group. The Libyans were at a loss. Without the Chadian's intimate knowledge of the terrain and conditions in the mountainous deserts of northern Chad, Libyan forces became sitting ducks.

Habré saw his chance. In an almost unbelievable turnaround following nearly fifteen years of extreme personal enmity, Habré's FANT agreed to link up with the remnants of Goukouni's GUNT forces and prepared to expel the Libyans from Chad. The joint forces attacked and retook Fada and then Zouar in early 1987. The FANT was able to inflict incredible damage on the Libyans, killing hundreds of soldiers and almost demolishing scores of tanks. In mid-March Libya lost its airbase at Ouadi Doum, which was completely destroyed when the FANT attacked, backed by French airpower and intelligence. It is thought that at least 1200 Libyan soldiers were killed. It was a stunning victory which led to the beginning of the Libyan withdrawal from Chad. Four years after they had arrived, the Libyans were chased inexorably by the FANT further and further north across the desert towards their rear bases in the Aouzou Strip. Habré refused to leave the job unfinished and in August 1987 his forces began a further attack on Aouzou, which pushed the Libyans into signing a ceasefire. Displaying his characteristic bravado, in the face of this crushing defeat Qaddafi announced that his Chad operation had been a success.

Superpower support

In late 1987, with the Libyans humiliated, Habré's grip on power seemed assured and Chad appeared relatively stable. The prowess of his FANT soldiers appeared to have been proven against all doubt. It almost seemed incredible that the rag-tag fighters of the FANT – soldiers of a country with a GDP of about $500 million in the early 1980s, screeching across the desert hanging off the back of lightly armed Toyota pick-up trucks – had so conclusively defeated the so-called professional army of an oil-producing nation which had earned $20 billion from oil production in 1980.[15] However, Habré's victory would not have been possible without the support of two of the world's great powers – France and the US – that he had enjoyed since the beginning of his rule.

France's involvement in Chad was no surprise. As the former colonial power, France had tried unsuccessfully on numerous occasions throughout the 1960s and 1970s to disentangle itself from Chad's political problems while at the same time maintaining its network of business links in the tradition of 'Françafrique', a name for the complex business and diplomatic relationships between France and its former West and Central African colonies. By the time Habré came to power in 1982, there was already a litany of desperate requests to France for assistance from all of Chad's post-independence leaders as each of them had faced dangerous times; some of these had been heeded and some ignored. In this sense Habré was no different to Chad's other leaders – France intervened militarily in the 1980s because Paris understood the immediacy of the danger and the potential consequences, and because French public opinion at that time had tolerated the increased spending and military commitments. And in fact that ambivalent relationship continues to this day. In 2008, French military jets provided aerial reconnaissance which helped Chad's current President Idriss Déby Itno to plan a counter-attack as he faced his own existential crisis from Toyota-riding desert rebels. But within months relations had soured, and Chad and the government of Nicolas Sarkozy were both calling for France's 1000-strong Operation Épervier to be scaled down. This policy performed yet another volte face in 2014 as Chad's role in combating Boko Haram in the Lake Chad basin became increasingly crucial, the government of President François Hollande announced that the French presence in Chad was once again to be stepped up. N'Djamena was confirmed as the head-quarters for France's significant new pan-Sahelian anti-terrorism deployment, Operation Barkhane. France has yet to fully extricate itself from its colonial past.

The French considerations about a response to Habré's increasingly desperate pleas for help as Goukouni's forces marched on N'Djamena in 1983 were ambivalent and influenced by the real-politik of the time. On the one hand there were strong economic ties with Libya that France did not want to break – France had good access to Libyan oil and was engaged in arms sales to Tripoli; but on the other hand the presence of Libyan troops on Chadian soil – without question France's traditional sphere of influence – annoyed France more and more as Qaddafi's predilection for stoking rebellions in Africa grew. Although in 1981 newly elected French President François Mitterrand had approved the sale of Mirage jets to Libya and at first seemed intent on maintaining diplomatic relations,[16] the clashes between the FANT and the Libyan military multiplied. France seemed to be inexorably drawn towards supporting its erstwhile colony. At first it seems French officials hoped that Goukouni Oueddei could dissociate himself from Libya, making the GUNT a more legitimate organisation. There is also evidence of covert military support: HRW reported that at one point during the battle of Faya Largeau in 1983, thirty-two French mercenaries had been sent to northern

Chad to support his forces with the knowledge of senior advisors to President Mitterrand including Jean-François Dubois.[17] But as Goukouni's failures mounted, France turned to measures such as the approval of Operations Manta, Épervier and the acceptance of the 16th parallel; these steps aimed to give Qaddafi a warning not to proceed further but did not seek to actively reverse the Libyan/GUNT gains. Although it has largely been concluded that France was no overt fan of Hissène Habré, there is little doubt that this continued French military involvement in Chad in the 1980s helped to keep him in power.

The United States policy on Habré, however, was much more fluid due to the superpower's relative inexperience in West and Central Africa in the early 1980s. In fact, the US had only a marginal interest for the first ten years of Chad's independence, with only a small embassy and USAID (United States Agency for International Development) office in N'Djamena which opened in the early 1960s. However when Ronald Reagan was elected US president in 1981, Habré's staunch opposition to Libya's occupation of northern Chad and his ongoing battles with the increasingly discredited GUNT had already been noticed in Washington. Reagan's hatred of Qaddafi was serious. In 1981, shortly after coming into office, Reagan broke off diplomatic relations with Libya and advised all Americans living there to leave. In the Cold War rhetoric of the age, Reagan was distrustful of Libya's meddling, the dangers his expansionist policy in Chad posed to pro-Western countries in Africa such as Sudan and Nigeria, his relationship with the Soviets and his apparent support of terrorism. Reagan was immediately interested in Habré's potential for stopping the Colonel's advance across Africa. This support from the US administration would last throughout Habré's presidency and would help him to become 'in essence, untouchable'.[18]

Along with the open support given to the OAU peace-keeping mission which deployed in N'Djamena in late 1981, the US launched its first clandestine operation under Reagan's new

CIA director, William Casey, who had run intelligence operations in the Second World War. In the early 1980s the US was
still reeling from the shock of the Iran hostage crisis in the aftermath of the Islamic Revolution, in which fifty American citizens
were held hostage for 444 days. American public opinion had
been horrified at the failed rescue bid that had led to the deaths
of eight American servicemen in a plane crash. This disaster
had been largely perceived as an intelligence failure by the CIA
(Central Intelligence Agency), which had seemed to miss the signs
of growing radical discontent with the Shah in Iran, and led to a
major refocus on improving intelligence gathering under Reagan.
According to Stephen Emerson, author of a book on covert CIA
operations, *Secret Warriors*:

> Reagan's terms in office marked a turning point for US
> intelligence. The new administration put great emphasis on
> rebuilding, then unleashing the CIA and other intelligence
> agencies. The intelligence budget became the fastest growing
> among all executive branch budgets; its $30bn budget in 1987
> represented a 200% increase over the 1980 level.[19]

The emphasis began to shift towards covert operations and
counter-terrorism operations which would not always be reported
to Congress.

In the early days of the Reagan administration, Libya was top
of the to-do list and seemed to offer the CIA a chance to rehabili-
tate its reputation. On his third day in office after the inauguration
in January 1981, Casey received an official document headed 'Libya
what to expect from Qaddafi in the coming months', says journalist
Bob Woodward, writing about the report: 'Qaddafi was no longer
an abstract problem: he was Casey's problem'. Key judgements
in the Libya report included, 'Qaddafi's recent success in Chad
ensures that his aggressive policies will pose a growing challenge to
US and western interests'. The prospect was 'more adventurism'.[20]

Casey, together with Secretary of State Alexander Haig, quickly came round to the idea of launching a covert war in partnership with Habré in order to stop Libyan aggression and 'bloody Qaddafi's nose'. Chad was viewed as Qaddafi's 'Achilles heel', an over-extension which could be exploited to bring down the leader and his delusions of grandeur. A HRW report aptly titled 'Enabling a Dictator', published in June 2016, details the issuing of a presidential finding, right at the beginning of Reagan's presidency in 1981 and which is still secret, which would authorise covert operations to bring Hissène Habré to power.[21] The operations were to be led by the CIA head of station in Khartoum, and initially involved shipping weapons and cash through Egypt and Sudan to Habré's rebel bases in Darfur.[22] Between late 1981 and 1982 the US funnelled $10 million in military aid to help it fight the Libyan-backed rebels.[23]

But it didn't stop there. According to journalist Michael Bronner, once Habré was in power, having defeated Goukouni in 1982, American government employees joined with CIA operatives to begin a flow of weapons and military advisors and trainers. This relationship was to continue until the end of Habré's rule in 1990. During this time, shipments included rifles, jeeps, stinger launchers, C140 transport planes and rocket-propelled grenades. In 1983 the assistance was markedly stepped up as Habré faced off Goukouni's Libyan-backed attack on Faya Largeau, with direct shipments of surface-to-air missiles and Toyotas mounted with machine guns. State Department and Defence Department officials visited Chad in 1983. Habré's FANT was also provided with aerial intelligence support from AWACS (Airborne Warning and Control System) surveillance planes and fighter jets based in Sudan, and throughout the 1980s Chad, the US and France regularly shared intelligence. In 1983, a small contingent of Zairean troops, again funded by the US,[24] was sent to Chad to help in the fight against Libya. Military assistance to Habré was delivered via several channels which included Foreign Military Sales (FMS), the Military Assistance Program (MAP) and the International Military Education and Training

Program (IMET), which included sending a number of Chadian students to the US for training.

In 1998, the US Congress was informed that the US authorities had

> provided $25 million in emergency military equipment and services under section 506(a) of the Foreign Assistance Act. Additional emergency aid was authorised in 1986 and 1987. These emergency funds and our MAP (Military Assistance Program) have enabled provision of three C-130A aircraft, ammunition, Redeye missiles, grenade launchers, rifles, four-wheel drive vehicles and support for previously acquired U.S. equipment.

The same document estimated that in 1983, 1984, 1985 and 1986 respectively, $7, $11, $4 and $6 million had been spent on 'military deliveries'.[25]

It has been estimated that the total amount of economic and military aid sent to Chad during the 1980s was $182 million; it is believed several more hundreds of millions were sent for the covert CIA operation.[26] Despite repeated requests for the release of certain documents under Freedom of Information requests, HRW concluded that 'many of the details of the US government's assistance still remain classified'.[27] At the same time, HRW was also unable to gain access to the French official archives for their research.[28]

The fruits of this assistance from France and the US came in 1987 when the FANT launched its devastating attack on the Libyan airbase at Ouadi Doum, signalling the beginning of the end of the 'Toyota' wars. Intelligence gathered by the US was shared directly with Habré and the weapons supplied by the US had played an important role. French airpower and aerial surveillance had backed up the FANT attack on the base. The defeat was resounding, and Qaddafi announced his retreat shortly afterwards. The US immediately promised another $10 million in military aid and

Assistant Secretary of State Richard Armitage visited Chad. In fact so delighted was Reagan with Habré's unlikely routing of the Libyan army that he asked to shake the Chadian president's hand in the White House. On 19 June 1987, five years after he became president, Habré met Reagan in Washington. The photographs of the meeting show a warmly smiling Reagan greeting Habré clad from head to foot in gleaming white robes with his trademark triangular hat, an arresting look similar to that which was to surface at his trial for war crimes in Dakar some twenty-eight years later. Habré, encircled by his coterie, looks pleased as punch, with his baby-faced features and untimely grey hair striking an incongruous contrast with his reputation as a brutal dictator. The US ambassador to Chad, John Propst Blane, said of the event in an oral history years later, 'It just went swimmingly. Mr. Habré and Mr. Reagan got along just dandily'.[29]

Complicity?

To what extent had the French and Americans known about Habré's human rights abuses, repression and poor treatment of prisoners of war as both superpowers embarked upon the programme of overt and covert military support? Certainly there was contemporaneous evidence of what he was capable of. There was of course *L'Affaire Claustre* from the 1970s (when Habré's loyalists had kidnapped the young French archaeologists), but also numerous newspaper reports in widely read publications detailing his actions. For example, in 1981 the *New York Times* reported on a mass grave found close to Habré's home in N'Djamena, which allegedly contained the bodies of hundreds of people executed by his forces during a recent round of fighting with the GUNT.[30]

Amnesty International prepared a series of twenty-three reports on the human rights situation in DDS prisons throughout the 1980s which were widely available. Researcher Mike Dottridge explained in great detail what Amnesty had revealed during that time at the Habré trial in Senegal in 2015.[31] These reports included detailed testimonies from individuals about torture methods such as *arba-tachar*, forced drinking of water and the 'baguettes'.[32] They also documented larger incidents, including an alleged killing of ninety Codos supporters, the disappearance of fifty-one people from the south in 1984, the burning of the village of Deli at the beginning of Black September and the unknown fates of thirty-eight people arrested in Abeche in 1983. In 1985, following the publication of a report on Black September, an Amnesty International team was able to make a single visit to Chad, where they came close to meeting Habré and became convinced that he was 'well briefed about [our] concerns'.[33] They were able to quiz Saleh Younouss, head of the DDS, directly about the fate of the missing thirty-eight from Abeche, although he claimed that most of these had been killed by FROLINAT rebels. Again in 1987 Amnesty published a report describing 400 political arrests and continued to provide detailed vignettes of individual cases of arbitrary arrests and extra-judicial killings, including ethnic Hadjerai and Zaghawa. In 1990 it published a report about the execution of prisoners and twenty-four civilians killed in Bahai, Tine and Iriba. As proof of how well these Amnesty reports were circulating, 17,000 letters of concern and 32,000 cards sent by Amnesty members to the DDS were found by Amnesty researchers when they were permitted to search the agency's archives in 1991.[34] The reports were sent to the UN human rights chief. In 1989 the Chadian authorities finally responded to Amnesty's reports, denying their involvement in torture and disap-pearances, and claiming that the organisation was mounting a deliberate campaign against the country.

Many of these Amnesty International reports were picked up by the international press including the *New York Times*; Amnesty researchers gave interviews to the BBC, Deutsche Welle and RFI. HRW Freedom of Information requests to publish diplomatic cables revealed that these reports were discussed between the US embassy and the State Department on several occasions.[35] Even the US State Department itself had issued reports outlining human rights abuses under Habré, such as one in 1982 that reported alleged cases of disappearances and summary executions and another in 1985 which described murder and pillage by rebel Codos soldiers and government troops, and a number of political killings and cases of torture. Mike Dottridge suggested that 'The USAID office in N'Djamena was right across the road from the DDS headquarters. It's very hard to conceive of them not knowing something of what had been going on there'.[36] However, by 1987, as Habré was shaking Reagan's hand in the White House, the wording in the annual State Department Human Rights Report (known as the 502b) had become more conciliatory 'violation of human rights due to war largely ended in 1987', and 'there were no verified instances of government-instigated political killings in 1987'.[37] This was despite the repression against the Hadjerai ethnic group which took place in 1987, and which was reported again by Amnesty International.

The decision to support him was certainly challenged by powerful figures. In the early 1980s, the US ambassador to Chad, Donald Norland, protested at the covert and overt support, saying that it was known that the FANT had committed atrocities in the south in 1979. According to journalist Bob Woodward, members of the Intelligence Committee of the US House of Representatives wrote a top-secret letter to Reagan protesting against the programme and its perceived intention to overthrow Qaddafi.[38] 'Some of the congressmen wondered whether Habré was the ideal choice to receive covert aid. From the left there were questions about his past involvement in massacres from the right some recalled his statements that he admired Mao, Castro and Ho Chi Minh'.[39] The members were concerned about a number of issues including some knowledge of human rights abuses carried out by Habré and his forces in previous battles. However, their concerns appear to have been overruled.

In supporting Habré, there appears to have been a tacit accept-ance by these world powers that his dubious reputation was a price worth paying if he was able to act as a proxy against Qaddafi, the most important consideration in Africa to Reagan and his policymakers in the 1980s. The seriousness of the Libyan threat was demonstrated by Reagan's authorisation of air strikes against Libya in 1985, calling Qaddafi the 'mad dog of the Middle East' after evidence emerged of Libya's involvement in the bombing of a discotheque in Berlin popular with American servicemen. France, although in some respects irked by the US's interventions in an area traditionally seen to be under the French sphere of influence, also seemed eventually willing to accept a certain amount of terrorisation of the Chadian population simply because Habré was deemed not to be as bad as Qaddafi. For both powers it was the classic shrugging of shoulders associated with the realpolitik of the day. This position is summed up by this quote given to Michael Bronner in his research for his article 'Our Man in Africa':

> Little to no attention was paid to the human rights issues at the time for three reasons … (1) We wanted the Libyans out and Habré was the only reliable instrument at our disposal, (2) Habré's record suffered only from the kidnapping (the Claustre Affair), which we were content to overlook, and (3) Habré was a good fighter, needed no training, and all we had to do was supply him with material.[40]

Furthermore, there is evidence that the US actually supported the activities of the DDS. The Chadian Truth Commission report written in 1993 detailed meetings between operatives of the DDS and advisors from the US embassy in N'Djamena. The report claimed that the US transferred 5 million FCFA (about $12,500) to the DDS each month throughout Habré's rule.[41] A document found by HRW in the abandoned headquarters of the DDS described a five-week training course that took place for twelve members of Chad's security forces near Washington in 1985, although the precise details of the training remain a mystery. Their curriculum included lectures on explosives, methods of investigation and intelligence gathering.[42] Former DDS operatives have told HRW they remember meeting CIA operatives and advisors from the US embassy, particularly a 'Mr Swiker' who, according the June 2016 HRW report 'Enabling a Dictator', appears to be George S. Swicker, the political and military counsellor at the US embassy in Chad in 1989–90. Saleh Younouss, former director of the DDS, also claimed at his trial in N'Djamena in 2014 that CIA agents from the US embassy and the French external security agency DGSE (Direction générale de la sécurité extérieure) had been in regular contact with him and had visited the DDS headquarters.[43]

There was also the bizarre story of the around 600 Libyan expatriates living in Chad whom the CIA had decided to train to form a 'fifth column' against Qaddafi in the later years of Habré's rule. These 'Contras' had been selected from the ranks of Habré's Libyan prisoners of war, most of whom were taken during the defeat at Ouadi Doum in 1987. There was hardly any prisoner exchange between Chad and Libya during the 1980s war, and only a fraction of the Libyan POWs in Chad were ever seen by the ICRC (International Committee of the Red Cross). It has been suggested that many may have died in captivity.[44] Some of these POWs selected for the Contra training publicly announced that they were joining an anti-Qaddafi faction, the FNSL (National Front for the Salvation of Libya), although there was some speculation at the time that many of them had been coerced and that Habré was able to use them to his advantage in negotiations with the Americans. Among them was Khalifa Haftar who was to resurface twenty-five years later as one of the most powerful eastern warlords opposing the Tripoli-based government in the chaos following the fall of Colonel Qaddafi.

According to French journalist Pierre Darcourt, the Contras had been held at a former French base and given training by US military advisors and Soviet weapons, but in fact the unit never saw any active combat against Qaddafi. The most difficult issue to resolve was what to do with them when Habré was ousted in 1990. As Idriss Déby's forces rolled into town, there was a hasty rush to get the Contras out, out of fear of an uncertain fate under Déby who had been supported by Qaddafi, and concerns that they would disclose details of the secret CIA training.[45] Darcourt travelled to the Am Simene camp outside N'Djamena just hours after they had left and reported 'flasks, canary yellow American tracksuits, transistor radios squashed underfoot ... all the signs of a hasty retreat'.[46] The Contras had been taken first to Nigeria, then Zaire and finally Kenya, although none of these countries wanted to accept them in the long term. During these stop-overs Libyan agents made repeated efforts to entice them to return home, and some of them did indeed go back. The issue was finally resolved when the US decided to give the remaining Contras asylum.

The extraordinary fall of Hissène Habré

In 1987, with the dramatic defeat of the Libyans and the coup of the Reagan handshake in the White House still fresh in everyone's mind, it looked as if Habré was untouchable. With the major source of rebellion in the north firmly extinguished and Goukouni Oueddei fading from the scene it was hard to imagine any other scenario than a continuation of Habré's rule, and with that the implicit assumption that the human rights abuses would continue. Even though the defeat at Ouadi Doum clearly qualified as a bloody nose for Colonel Qaddafi, it was not mission complete and the US did not seem to deem it necessary to significantly reduce the amount of its support for Chad. The French did not pull out the Operation Épervier force and continued diplomatic support. In 1988 the Chadian government announced a record harvest, removing an obvious source of social discontent. Chad looked as if it could finally be on the road to peace.

However things are never that simple in Chad. What appears to be permanent and established can vanish into the desert sands in a flash. Once again the country's extreme precariousness and the fundamental weakness of its governing institutions were about to be exposed. Just as the dust settled on the Libyan retreat, yet another rebellion broke out in Chad. This time it was the turn of the Hadjerai community, a group which lives in the central Guera region, and which had traditionally been close to Habré and had even supported his bid for power in 1982. Tensions had grown after the death in 1984 of one of the most prominent members of the Hadjerai community, Idriss Miskene, who had briefly been a minister under Habré and who it was rumoured was becoming dangerously popular in Habré's eyes.[47] Despite an official enquiry finding that his death had been of natural causes, relations deteriorated between the president and the Hadjerai community. Protests broke out in April 1987 following an incident between members of the Gorane and Hadjerai communities in N'Djamena, which put wind in the sails of a secret armed rebel group MOSANAT (Movement for the National Salvation of Chad) that had been formed by Hadjerai politician Maldoum Abbas along with Gali Gata Ngothe (a former advisor to Habré) and Haroun Godi. Government troops and DDS agents were sent to restore order, and in another brutal wave of repression villages were burned and an unknown number of Hadjerai were arbitrarily arrested or executed.

However, Habré's most serious challenge came from a former commander of the FANT and presidential military advisor, Idriss Déby, who is still Chad's president. Déby is from the Bideyat sub-clan of the Zaghawa, a non-Arabic speaking people who roamed the grassland and plateaus south of the Sahara. Déby was born the son of shepherd in Fada in Ennedi in 1952, and after flight training in France he went on to be one of Habré's most loyal and talented lieutenants and commander in chief of the army, leading battles against Goukouni and Kamougue's forces throughout the 1980s. However, by 1989 Déby's own ambitions were growing. He defected from the army with two of the most important figures in Habré's government, Ibrahim Muhammad Itno, Minister of the Interior and Hassan Djamous, a later commander in chief of the army. All three were Zaghawa who had finally grown tired of Habré's repressive rule and felt their loyalty had not been adequately rewarded. A planned coup against Habré was uncovered and the president ordered their arrests. The group immediately launched a lightning strike against the presidential palace which was defeated by Habré's mainly Toubou presidential guard. The rebels escaped with the FANT in hot pursuit, but on the way Hassan Djamous, who had been seriously wounded in the battle, died. Ibrahim Muhammad Itno was arrested and died in jail several days later. But Déby, for whom this was just the first test of his remarkable ability to survive when the odds seem insanely stacked against him, was able to reach the safety of his bases over the border in Darfur, where he created his Patriotic Salvation Movement (MPS). He was warmly welcomed by the Libyans, who since the 1987 defeat had moved some of their operations to western Sudan with the apparent tacit approval of the Sudanese authorities.

It was then the turn of the Zaghawa ethnic group to be targeted for the betrayal. It began with the families of those involved in the coup, but soon extended to the wider community. Hundreds of people across the country were seized in raids, tortured and killed.[48] According to HRW, a special commission in the DDS was created to target first the Hadjerai, and then the Zaghawa.[49] Déby, incensed by the reprisals and burning with ambition, regrouped his forces and began his long march to N'Djamena in March 1990, backed by a small contingent of Libyan troops and weaponry. His MPS first attacked Biltine and Iriba, but was initially driven back by a counter-attack led by Habré himself which reached deep inside Sudanese territory. After the initial defeat, Déby was taken by Libyan plane to Tripoli, but by September the fighting had begun again. In November, MPS troops crossed the border and overran Tine, Guereda and Koulbous. At this point it seems the French made a tactical decision not to stop Déby's advance on N'Djamena. Although they had been willing to tolerate Habré as long as he had so doggedly battled Qaddafi, at this crucial moment it seems their true feelings about the Chadian president emerged. There was thus little standing in Déby's way. Using the same desert warfare in Toyota tactics that he had perfected as Habré's own army chief, Déby pushed his troops through Abeche in the east, and they screeched on west through the desert in lightly armed pick-ups, covering some 1000 kilometres on unpaved roads in a matter of days, often travelling at night with their headlights switched off.

Although by the end of the 1980s there was a perception that US support for Habré was beginning to cool as evidence of his human rights abuses mounted, it had not yet ended. In fact US officials were ready to support him until the last moment, even long after France had stood aside as the seemingly unstoppable momentum of the Déby insurgency swept the country. Richard Bogosian, who took over as US ambassador to Chad in 1990 remarked after his posting that the debate taking place in Washington during those tumultuous last few weeks agreed that 'Habré was worth saving'.[50] Just days before his fall, the US had reiterated its willingness to share intelligence on Déby's movements. The night before Déby's forces arrived, US diplomatic staff in N'Djamena had spoken urgently to Washington, which offered to send two C141 transport planes with ammunition and weapons to assist in the defence of N'Djamena. According to journalist Michael Bronner,[51] in a panic embassy staff and CIA staff had begun to shred classified documents that might have contained sensitive information about US operations during Habré's rule.

However, in the end it was all too late. Habré knew better than anyone when the writing was on the wall, having perfected the art of Toyota warfare rebellion himself in the early 1980s. On the night of 30 November 1990, as his terrified loyalists jumped into cars and crossed the border to Cameroon, Richard Bogosian told Washington not to bother sending the planes. In another bizarre twist, three companies of French paratroopers arrived at N'Djamena airport that same night but seemed unable to stop the overthrow.

The FANT defences of the capital dissolved, and Habré hastily prepared to leave his home country forever. One of his last acts was to call the head of the national treasury to force him to sign an order to hand over around 3.5 billion CFCA (French Community of Africa Francs; roughly US$6.4 million) which was taken out from Chad's national account at the BEAC (Banque des Etats d'Afrique Centrale).[52] Mahamat Hassan Abakar, the head of Chad's Truth Commission which was set up in 1990 to investigate Habré's crimes (see Chapter 2), still has a copy of the original cheque which authorised the withdrawal.[53] According to Abakar, Habré took this money, gold bullion, carpets and even his cooking pots and left with his family at around two o'clock in the morning, crossing the Chari into Cameroon where they had a cargo plane waiting. French journalist Pierre Darcourt described having seen 'around 10 US "advisors" wearing dark glasses' accompanying the leaving party.[54] On the night of 1 December, Idriss Déby and his MPS fighters rode triumphantly into the streets of the capital, meeting little resistance and in some areas greeted by cheering crowds. In the following days, Déby opened up Habré's detention centres and the inmates poured out, bringing with them the terrible secrets of their incarceration.

As Chadians blinked in the dawn of a new regime, still fearful that with Chad's unending precariousness Habré might yet stage a come-back, it seems the US quietly concluded that nothing could be done to save their man in Africa. There was to be no more military support and no face-off with Chad's new president. Although there would be a few intermittent skirmishes with Habré loyalists in the coming years, it really did seem that it was over. Given all the bloody battles of the 1980s, it is hard not to wonder why Habré seemed to have given up so easily. Pierre Darcourt says that former ambassador Bogosian told him that he believed (rather gracefully) that it was because the former president had wanted to avoid mass casualties in N'Djamena in a fruitless battle with Déby's superior forces. Perhaps Habré really was in awe of Idriss Déby, but there was just one last favour – Reed Brody claims that US officials may have leant on the Senegalese President Abdou Diouf to allow Habré refuge.[55]

Whatever the reason, Habré was gone and it was now time to deal with Déby. Had it all been worth it? All things considered, a relatively small sum had been spent by the US to give Qaddafi his bloody nose, and the underdog African challenger had won. Habré appeared to have provided a very effective service and had been at liberty to carry out his own repressive political programme. For the last two years of Habré's rule at least, 'The Libyan leader ... had a hostile French and US supported government along the 600-mile border to the south', which would for a time dampen the Colonel's ambitions in Sahelian Africa.[56] But as history showed, although Habré was gone, Qaddafi was by no means finished. He would go on to terrorise Libyans, interfere in African affairs, sponsor terrorism and meddle in international conflicts for the next twenty-one years.

Chapter 2

THE LONG ROAD TO DAKAR

As Idriss Déby set about consolidating his grip on power in Chad following the coup, Hissène Habré was forced to get used to a very different life. According to the memoir of Abdou Diouf, president of Senegal from 1981 to 2000, Habré's bid for exile in Senegal had been at the insistence of Cameroon's president Paul Biya, who had telephoned Diouf late at night on the day of Habré's fall. Fleeing over the border, Habré had arrived in the Cameroonian town of Maroua in hasty exile, with an aircraft stolen from the Chadian army packed with trunks full of cash which he had looted from the Chadian treasury, carpets and even his family's cooking pots. Biya had been concerned that Habré's presence in Cameroon could be destabilising, especially if he was inclined to attempt a come-back. Biya had tried several other African leaders in vain. Eventually Diouf agreed, with the condition that 'He must live out his political exile with discretion, which means excluding himself from all mixing in Chad's domestic affairs', as well as not supporting any armed rebellions in opposition to Déby. In his memoirs, Diouf says that he was informed that Habré would be arriving on his own plane at 6am the following day.[1] The stolen plane would have to be returned later.

Abdou Diouf claims to have known nothing of what Habré had been accused of in the 1980s,[2] and with enough on his plate to deal with in Chad, Idriss Déby appeared to raise no objections to his exile in Senegal. Habré settled down to a quiet and genteel life. He was accorded all the respect and friendship to be expected for a former

head of state and was ushered discreetly to Dakar's Ouakam neighbourhood, a plush suburb close to the sea where foreign diplomats
live in tranquillity in vast mansions. He was to stay here for twenty-
three years. In Ouakam, he lived out a quiet exile, described again
and again as a polite neighbour, a good and observant Muslim, who
kept a low profile but was known to support the community particularly during religious holidays. He became close to the Tidianiya
Sufi Muslim brotherhood which has a wide network of supporters
in Senegal and a degree of political influence. He funded the local
Ouakam football team and also reportedly made good contacts at a
number of local newspapers. It was an image incongruous with his
former persona – it was hard to imagine how the plotting, paranoid
dictator signing death warrants, a ruthless, Toyota-driving desert
warrior born to a nomad shepherd, could so easily have transformed
himself into an urbane, well-dressed local gentleman. The 1992
Chad Commission of enquiry called it 'his congenital duplicity.'[3]

It seems that the Senegalese assumed he was there to stay.
According to one contemporaneous Senegalese minister, little was
known of the real nature of Habré's rule in Chad, he was rather
welcomed with hospitality as a refugee, as a 'former African leader
who had been deposed by an armed rebellion'.[4] At this point in
history, he was not alone in his need to call in the favours. In the
early 1990s, a number of despotic and failed African leaders were
toppled and went on the find protection in other African countries. Haile Mariam Mengistu, who presided over Ethiopia's 'Red
Terror' and may have been responsible for the deaths of more than
500,000 people during his rule, was whisked off to Zimbabwe after
being overthrown in 1991. Despite an Ethiopian court finding him
guilty of genocide in absentia, he still lives out a reportedly luxu-
rious exile in Harare. Siad Barre fled Mogadishu to Kenya in 1991
after being overthrown following his dictatorial rule of Somalia
and destruction of the northern city of Hargeisa, and eventually
ended up in exile in Nigeria. Sierra Leone's Joseph Momoh fled
to Guinea after being overthrown in 1992. Certainly in the first

few years following Habré's flight there seemed very little realistic prospect of his Senegalese hosts exposing him to the danger of being held to account for the human rights abuses carried out in Chad during the 1980s.

Indeed it has been claimed by various human rights activists in Chad and Senegal that he was tacitly allowed to consolidate his position. Using the millions of CFCA pillaged from the Chadian treasury, and apparently keeping his promises not to embarrass his hosts, it has been claimed that Habré began to invest in a number of local businesses and find ways to securely hide his money including setting up a number of bank accounts. According to Alioune Tine, who in the 1990s worked for the Senegalese human rights organisation RADDHO (African Grouping for the Defence of Human Rights – from the French Rencontre Africaine pour la Défence des Droits de l'Homme) and is currently director of Amnesty International's West Africa branch, Habré was able to invest in a number of large properties in the Ouakam neighbourhood. He was reportedly well-connected. HRW and Alioune Tine believe that Abdoul Mbaye, one of Senegal's most prominent bankers in the 1980s through his role running Banque de l'Habitat de Sénégal, was one of the former president's investment advisors. Mbaye was later to become the first Prime Minister of Senegal under Macky Sall. The chief prosecutor at the Habré trial in Dakar in 2015, Mbacké Fall, was keen to get Mbaye to testify about Habré's financial dealings but was unable to. Madické Niang, Foreign Minister under Senegal's president during the 2000s Abdoulaye Wade, was for a time one of Hissène Habré's lawyers. 'There was a network of contacts in Senegal that helped to persuade (Senegal's new president) Abdoulaye Wade to continue to protect Habré. The protection of the "community" of African presidents was a very important concept to him', says Alioune Tine.[5]

These claims are interesting, but at least on the financial side, to date very little concrete proof of Habré's investments in Senegal has ever been found. HRW launched an investigation into the so-called 'missing millions' in response to the failure to pay compensation to his victims at the conclusion of his trial in 2016, but at the time of writing nothing substantive has been found. Alioune Tine also concedes that the paper trail is flimsy. In fact the money may well have been so well hidden that when the EAC tried to seize his assets, they found only a few hundred-thousand dollars in Senegalese bank accounts and a few properties. This theme will be more thoroughly examined in Chapter 3.

The search for justice

Chadian Truth Commission

Back in Chad, at first the signs of a prospect of justice for the DDS victims during the 1980s looked hopeful. One of Déby's first acts in power was to open the doors of the nationwide network of secret jails and release the inmates. On 29 December 1990, less than a month after his coup, Déby created by presidential decree the 'Commission of Enquiry into the Crimes and Misappropriations Committed by Ex-President Habré, His Accomplices and/or Accessories' (the 'Truth Commission'), charged with collecting evidence and testimony from victims in order to investigate 'illegal detentions, assassinations, disappearances, torture, mistreatment, other attacks on the physical and mental integrity of persons; plus all violations of human rights, illicit narcotics trafficking and embezzlement of state funds between 1982 and 1990'.[6] Chad's 'Truth Commission' was composed of twelve members, including policemen, judges and the country's chief prosecutor, and was given a total budget of 4.8 million CFCA and six months to prepare its report. Despite getting off to a rather inauspicious start – the commission was unable to find a suitable office and ended up settling in the former DDS headquarters in N'Djamena – it was able to get down to work in early 1991.

I went to meet Mahamat Hassan Abakar in his legal practice in downtown N'Djamena in January 2017. Just a few years ago the roads in this part of the city were a quagmire of mud and rubbish, but since oil money started rushing into Chad the whole area has been transformed, with tarmac paving and street-lighting installed. Abakar's practice is still in an old building, and I had to blink in the darkness as I stepped in from the dazzling light outside to see a huge pile of yellowing files on his desk and a dusty, broken computer. In the early 1990s, Abakar was an ambitious young lawyer working at the Ministry of Justice when he was nominated for the politically-sensitive job as the Truth Commission chairman. 'My family really didn't want me to do the job', says Abakar, now an avuncular character, who wears a classic Chadian 'Mao' style suit and has grey sprinkled through his hair and beard. He continues: 'It was exhausting and emotional work. We had to dig up mass graves, witness horrific injuries and speak to people who were deeply traumatised. Back then the events were still very close in people's lives. You can't get over that sort of thing easily'.[7]

The Commission reported a number of difficulties in carrying out its work, most notably that victims were reluctant to speak out for fear of reprisals or that, based on his past form, Habré was likely to try to regain power. The commissioners were also hampered by their inability to travel to all of the remote interior regions of the country – roads were few and far between and two vehicles given to the commission were stolen in the first few months of its activity. In the early months after Habré's fall, a number of his loyalists staged lightning attacks on remote outposts in eastern Chad. Several former DDS agents, now 'rehabilitated' into a newly formed General Directorate of the Centre for Investigation and Intelligence Co-ordination, were reluctant to give testimony and even tried to intimidate former victims. Furthermore, some of the original Commission members felt unable to carry out the work and another decree was issued in July 1991 to reorganise the commission members when several of the original employees resigned.

Despite these political and administrative delays, the Commission did finally produce its report on 7 May 1992. Its conclusions

...ark: that 'a veritable genocide' had been committed against the Chadian people, and that all ethnic groups except Habré's own Gorane had been targeted. Through its interviews carried out across the country, the Commission recorded 3780 dead, of which twenty-six were foreigners, and that 54,000 people had been arrested. This figure included executed prisoners of war, but did not include enemy combatants killed during fighting. The Commission concluded that because so many people were intimidated into not testifying and it had struggled to reach all corners of the country, it had only been able to ascertain about 10% of the total number of people killed. It therefore estimated that the total number of dead could be as high as 40,000. The Commission also reported hundreds of cases of people being thrown out of their homes or having their possessions confiscated by the DDS.

In attempting to lay out a path to healing in Chad, the report made a number of recommendations including the establishment of real democracy and a sovereign judiciary, the creation of a National Human Rights Commission and, significantly, 'the prosecution without delay of the authors of this horrible genocide, who are guilty of crimes against humanity'. It concluded by calling on the new head of state to 'take all necessary steps to punish anyone found guilty of human rights abuses'.[8]

It was an extraordinarily frank conclusion and perhaps reflects how much early optimism there had been with the new government of Idriss Déby, who appeared to want to sweep away all vestiges of Habré's eight years of terror. Unfortunately this optimism was misplaced, and a lot of the Truth Commission's work was to fall on deaf ears. Few of its recommendations were implemented satisfactorily. Although Déby did make requests to Senegal to repatriate Habré for trial, little was done to deal with the day-to-day torturers, many of whom were re-employed in the newly formed General Directorate of the Centre for Investigation and Intelligence Co-ordination which had replaced the dismantled DDS. These figures including Saleh Younouss, the former head of the DDS, and Mahamat Djibrine (known as El Djonto) continued to live at liberty in N'Djamena until 2015. No trials for human rights abuses during the 1980s were carried out. Chad did sign up to a number of international conventions on human rights in 1996 and a National Human Rights Commission was created in 1994, but the body suffered from political interference and a lack of funding.[9]

'No-one expected our report to lead to anything', concedes Mahamat Hassan Abakar phlegmatically. 'We felt our goal was to immortalise the suffering of the victims, and to me it seemed clear that Déby didn't really want a trial of Habré. Nevertheless we were still proud of what we did'.[10]

Political difficulties

Chad's problems did not go away. The desperate challenges of governing such a large and poor country meant that before long authoritarian tendencies and the favouring of certain ethnic groups began to re-emerge. Just as Habré had so successfully saved the trappings of power for his Gorane kinsmen, this time it was the turn of Déby's Zaghawa clan to eat at the trough, a situation which reignited the same struggles for power which had haunted the 1980s. In the years after toppling Habré, Déby went on to promote scores of his family members and Zaghawa kinsmen to positions of power in politics and business. Just like the Gorane before them, the 'Zags' gained a reputation for being above the law in N'Djamena and the seeds of resentment were sown among other groups. Within months of his takeover, myriad new rebel groups opposed to Zaghawa dominance had materialised.

A number of attacks by Habré loyalists in 1991 were brutally suppressed with allegations of arbitrary executions.[11] Déby struggled to control his loyalist soldiers who rampaged through the remote regions of Chad with arms which had begun circulating during the 1980s. In October 1991 it was reported that up to forty people, mostly ethnic Hadjerai, were executed by soldiers loyal to

Déby after the discovery of an alleged coup plot. Later that year, after fears that crime levels were rising, four people who had been subject to an 'unfair trial' for robbery and other offences were executed in public in N'Djamena. Although Amnesty International was able to carry out a visit to Chad to report on Habré-era abuses, the first visit since 1985, this did nothing to end the arbitrary arrests, detention without trial (often incommunicado) and torture in prisons which continued to be reported across the country.[12] It was worse in 1992. 'Hundreds of unarmed civilians and prisoners were victims of extrajudicial executions by government security forces' reported Amnesty International.[13] Another Habré-loyal group, the MDD (Movement for Democracy and Development), had emerged in the Lake Chad area, and 'gross human rights abuses' were again reported as government troops acted with impunity as they battled for control. Moves to quash a southern rebellion later that year led by Moise Kette, a disgraced former leader of the MPS, saw allegations that government forces had killed 150 civilians in the southern town of Doba. The rebel groups were also responsible for exactions against civilians. During this time, journalists and human rights activists were targeted, including Joseph Behidi, the Vice President of the Chadian Human Rights League, who was killed apparently in connection with his decision to defend a newspaper in a defamation case brought by the army. Right up until the present day, it has remained standard practice in Chad to arrest and detain without trial those alleged to have been involved in coup plots, and even as late as 2008, it was not unheard of for political figures accused of cooperation with rebel movements to disappear without trace.

Nevertheless, Déby did try to enact some political reform. In March 1991 a National Charter was passed for a thirty-month transitional period to be followed by a constitutional referendum, which would pave the way for the establishment of multi-party democracy. Déby invited political exiles to return from abroad and allowed the formation of new political parties. However, the MPS was exempt from the conditions required for the registration of political parties and by the end of 1991 no new parties had been formed. Throughout the 1990s journalists, opposition figures, trade union activists and those suspected of supporting rebel groups continued to be harassed by the security services, and reports continued of arbitrary arrests and detentions. In 1996 Amnesty International published a report entitled 'Empty Promises' which accused the government of not doing enough to protect human rights; it also called on foreign governments to ensure that any equipment or skills transfer to the Chadian security forces was not to be used to commit human rights abuses.

It was to take until 1996 for the constitutional referendum to be held, which was supported by 63.5% of the population. This paved the way for Chad's first democratic elections to be held in June 1996, pitting the old southern stalwart Wadel Kamogue against the revolutionary hero Idriss Déby. The vote was able to progress without significant problems, although a number of opposition figures such as Ngarlejy Yorongar were arrested. Déby won the vote in the second round with 69.1% of votes. Legislative elections, which established a 125-seat National Assembly, were postponed until early 1997 and Déby's party, the MPS, won an absolute majority of seats. The political bickering continued, with ministers resigning in protest at Déby's rule, and opposition parties claiming that they had been hampered from carrying out their activities. Amnesty International reported torture and inhumane conditions in Chad's jails and the order from the director of the Gendarmerie that criminals could be executed if caught committing a crime.[14] In 1998 a new and much more serious rebellion broke out in the BET, Chad's long-standing Achilles heel. It was known as the MDJT (Movement for Democracy and Justice in Chad) and was led by Youssef Togoimi who had been dismissed as Minister of Defence. A number of old battle-axes from Frolinat including Acheikh Ibn Oumar dusted off their fatigues and joined forces with the MDJT, and yet again the north of Chad was hit by the latest round of destructive Toyota wars.

As Chad stumbled forward on a precarious path to multi-party democracy, rife with rebellions, coup plots and dangerous rivalries, the objective of putting the past to rights began to slip off the agenda. The report of the Truth Commission lay on a shelf gathering dust, Habré was settling into his reincarnation as a genteel pillar of the Muslim community in Ouakam, and scores of Habré-era lieutenants found their way into new jobs and positions of power. These included one of the most feared torturers of the DDS, Mahamat Djibrine (El Djonto), who went on to become the head of Chad's police,[15] and Toke Dadi, the last director of the DDS who was eventually named as Governor of Sila region.[16]

Grassroots justice

Habré's crimes had not been forgotten by everyone. Enter Souleymane Guengueng and Clement Abaifouta, two modest Chadians who were to change the course of Habré's life. In 1988 Souleymane Guengueng was working as an official at the Lake Chad Basin Commission in N'Djamena. One morning his wife came to his office in tears; the DDS had been to her house looking for him. Before Guengueng had chance to escape, DDS agents arrived at his office. Taken to the DDS offices, he was accused of having provided shelter to anti-Habré figures while the Lake Chad Basin Commission had temporarily been located in Cameroon. Although Guengueng denied the allegations, as with most of those arrested by the DDS he had no recourse to justice. He disappeared into the DDS prison system for more than two years until Habré was toppled in 1990. In jail Guengueng was variously held in solitary confinement and then terribly overcrowded conditions. He caught malaria, hepatitis and dengue fever and his sight was irreparably damaged by being held in total darkness for extended periods. He was hung by the testicles by prison guards after being caught leading prayers for prisoners,[17] and like all ex-inmates saw scores of his fellow prisoners die: 'If there were more than ten dead on a morning the prison director would order them to be removed; but only if it was more than ten', he later recalled.[18] To this day he still walks v following the terrible conditions in jail.

During one of his darkest moments in prison, Souleymane Guengueng had promised himself that if he ever escaped alive he would dedicate his life to telling the truth to the world about Habré's prison. Perhaps to no greater surprise than his own, in December 1990 he staggered out into the light as Déby's forces moved into N'Djamena. As the reality of Habré's total defeat and the verifiable dismantlement of the worst aspects of the dictator's terror system began to sink in, this deeply religious man set up the Chadian Association of Victims of Political Repression and Crime (AVCRP) and quietly set about collecting the testimonies of nearly 800 fellow victims of the DDS prison system throughout the 1980s, which documented abuses mostly carried out during the ethnically targeted campaigns of the latter years of Habré's rule. It was the beginning of a remarkable 'grassroots' justice campaign which was to become central in building the case against Habré fifteen years later in Dakar.

Guengueng was joined in his mission by Clement Abaifouta, who at the age of twenty-three had been arrested and taken to a DDS prison. His crime appeared to have been his winning of a scholarship to study abroad (which he was never able to take up), although he suspects that the real reason was because the DDS suspected him of links to the political opposition, which he still denies. He spent four years in a DDS prison where his main role was to bury his dead cellmates at a site just outside of N'Djamena. He estimated he buried at least 500 people between 1985 and 1989. I first met Clement in 2008 when he came to meet me in the lobby of the new Chinese hotel 'Chez Wu' in N'Djamena with news of a press conference with Habré's victims. Wearing a football shirt and carrying a laptop computer, my first impression was that he was still a dynamic, muscular man. I remember listening to him earnestly, but at the back of my mind wondering if his cause was lost; on closer examination it was possible to see in his slightly stooped stance how the years of incarceration and seemingly fruit-less struggles had sapped his soul. In 2017 he still spends a lot of of his time at his house in N'Djamena where he lives with his dog, 'CPI' (Cour Pénale Internationale – International Criminal Court), a name he got from Souleymane Guengueng's dog. He tells me more about his fight:

> My motivation for carrying on this fight for justice twenty-six years at the expense of everything in my personal life was just to answer that one question; why was I arrested? I was so revolted by the experience I had to have an answer. Why ruin my life and that of so many others?

For many years Clement has suffered from depression and post-traumatic stress: 'Unfortunately even after the trial in Dakar I still don't know the answer. Hissène Habré refused to reveal anything. I still feel like half a man'.[19]

Souleymane and Clement suffered years of harassment and intimidation by the Chadian authorities as they tried to carry out their work. Their phones were tapped, they were followed by shady characters from the security services and their offices were raided. Clement was arrested five times. The harassment would in the end prove too much for Souleymane, who fled to political exile in the US in 2003, leaving Clement in charge of the Chad branch of the AVCRP. Clement believes this campaign of intimidation was carried out by former DDS agents from the 1980s who knew about their work. For several years Guengueng had kept the hand-written witness testimonies carefully hidden in his home for fear that former Habré associates would get wind of his campaign, although he had no clear plan for how they would ever be used. 'I think they knew we had that dossier', says Clement of the intimidation and harassment. 'They wanted to shut us up.'

Africa's Pinochet

In 1999 a remarkable thing happened. An ambitious young lawyer working for HRW, Reed Brody, had been sent to London to advise the prosecution in the case of the former Chilean dictator Augusto Pinochet, who had just been arrested on suspicion of human rights abuses. In this case, General Pinochet had been arrested in October 1998 as he arrived in Britain using the principle of universal jurisdiction which has been developed to ensure there is no 'safe haven' for those responsible for the most serious crimes. HRW defines universal jurisdiction as 'The principle that every state has an interest in bringing to justice the perpetrators of particular crimes of international concern, no matter where the crime was committed, and regardless of the nationality of the perpetrators or their victims'.[20]

The British police were acting on an arrest warrant issued by a Spanish judge charging the former president with human rights crimes committed during the 1970s and 1980s in Chile; an official truth commission had detailed over 2000 cases of killings and disappearances. Pinochet challenged the arrest on the grounds that he enjoyed immunity as a former head of state, but the British House of Lords twice rejected this claim as they argued this did not cover cases of torture and abuse. The attempts to extradite Pinochet were hailed as a breakthrough by some human rights activists, but in the end the former dictator escaped prosecution after a medical examination deemed that he was mentally unfit to stand trial. The then British Home Secretary Jack Straw overturned a House of Lords ruling to extradite him to Spain to stand trial, and in March 2000 he returned home to Chile where he later died.

The doctrine of universal jurisdiction has its roots in international law but historically had been used infrequently, with governments only invoking the principle in cases such as hijacking and piracy where crimes were committed between national jurisdictions. It can only be used if national governments have passed legislation to implement any international treaties against such crimes. Coming just months after the Rome Conference which concluded the statute of the new ICC, the Pinochet case caused some consternation at government level that international justice was spinning out of the control of states. Although it did not ultimately result in a conviction, for Reed Brody the Pinochet experience presented some tantalising opportunities. He began to wonder who might be next.

'My motivation was ideological', says Brody, who wears a characteristic college scarf and keeps his hair shoulder-length and somewhat dishevelled. 'We wanted to create other Pinochets. It is hard to over-estimate the impact of this case on the international human rights movement. It was like a moment of effervescence.'[21]

On the recommendation of a colleague at Harvard Law School, Brody began to look into the case of Habré. 'At that time I didn't really know who Hissène Habré was', says Brody. But in fact, the case would end up taking over his life for the next sixteen years. His interest piqued, Brody was able to persuade two students on Harvard's human rights programme to travel to Chad to see what they could find. Through Delphine Djiraibe, one of Chad's first female lawyers, the students were sent to meet Souleymane Guengueng, and he happily showed them his collection of testimonies. When the students realised the magnitude of what Guengueng had done, they agreed to a high-risk plan to spirit copies of the documents out of Chad and back to the US in their suitcases. Despite a nerve-wracking experience at N'Djamena's airport on the way home, where for a few tense minutes the students feared that their luggage was about to be searched, they managed to smuggle the documents out of Chad.[22]

Brody and HRW also made contact with the Chadian Association for the Promotion and Defence of Human Rights (APTDH), led by the formidable Chadian lawyer Jacqueline Moudeina, who had asked for their help with the case. Moudeina had fled Chad during fighting in 1979, and during her exile had studied law in Congo-Brazzaville. She returned to Chad in 1995 and began to work with the victims of Habré and the secret police. In 2001 she was participating in a peaceful demonstration outside the French embassy in N'Djamena when she was severely injured by a grenade thrown when the police were ordered to disperse the protestors. It took her over a year to recover.

On receiving the smuggled documents, Brody was quick to realise the immense potential they contained. Within months, the Chadian victims, assisted by HRW, were ready to file a criminal complaint representing eight individual plaintiffs in Dakar, Senegal, accusing Habré of torture, barbaric acts and crimes against humanity. They were supported by international and national NGOs and Senegalese lawyers. Habré was accused of torture and crimes against humanity, with the charges being based on 'the Senegalese statute on torture as well as the 1984 United Nations Convention Against Torture (UNCAT), which Senegal ratified in 1987. The groups also cited Senegal's obligations under customary international law to prosecute those accused of crimes against humanity'.[23] On 3 February 2000, Judge Demba Kandji indicted Habré for torture, crimes against humanity and barbaric acts, and he was placed under house arrest. It was the first time that an African had been charged with atrocities by the court of another African country.[24] Suddenly the case hit international headlines and Habré's cosy exile looked to be under threat.

However the early optimism was to prove short-lived. Habré's lawyers challenged the judgment, and by June, in a clear example of how political will or lack of it can influence the outcome of judicial process, the Superior Council of Magistrates, presided over by Senegal's President Abdoulaye Wade, who had beaten Abdoulaye Diouf in a presidential election earlier in 2000, announced that Judge Kandji was to be transferred. In July, the Appeals Court dismissed the indictment ruling that Senegalese courts had no jurisdiction to pursue the case because the crimes had not been committed in Senegal.[25] The case was finally rejected at the Supreme Court of Appeals (Cour de Cassation) in 2001.

During this time, Wade made public statements that Habré would never be tried on Senegalese soil, and in fact his obstruction of the case would go on to become a major sticking point in all future attempts to prosecute Habré until the EAC was established. The Appeals court decision was a disappointing blow for the victims' groups, which had relied on the fact that the Senegalese constitution allowed for the automatic application of the UN Convention against Torture, and that the country prided itself on being a leading light in international human rights and the first country to ratify the treaty establishing the International Criminal Court. 'The 2000 decision in Senegal was a big disappointment', says Younous Mahadji, today a doctor at N'Djamena's main Hôpital de Référence, who was arrested by the DDS in 1990 after handing out pamphlets denouncing Habré. He was jailed for four months, lost half his body weight and still bears the scars of 'arbatachar' on his upper arms. He was among the first complainants in the 2000 Senegal case. 'But we realised this was high politics. I think our move scared all African presidents including Abdoulaye Wade. They realised that they could find themselves in the same situation.'[26] This is a view reflected by Konstantinos D. Magliveras from the University of the Aegean:

> Senegal [was in] a very tight spot; on the one hand it wanted to maintain the reputation of a state subscribing to fundamental freedoms ... and did not want to become embroiled in the criminal prosecution of a former dictator who had ... also been given, without many questions asked, a new home in its territory.[27]

The victims' groups were not easily deterred. In October 2000, seventeen victims filed criminal complaints in Chad for torture, murder and 'disappearance' against Habré's accomplices, including former directors, heads of department and other agents of the DDS. The victims detailed crimes including disappearances and the use of *arbatachar*, the forced drinking of water and electric shocks. It was an extremely bold move, given the fact that many of the former DDS operatives were still living at liberty in Chad and that Déby had been such a high-ranking figure under Habré. It appears that the victims had been emboldened by the developments in Senegal and by a meeting a few weeks earlier with Déby himself who had told them 'the time for justice has come'.[28] However, yet again the victims' optimism was misplaced and nothing came of the complaint. It was to be another fifteen years before any Habré-era figure would face any charges in Chad itself.

A few months after the Chad complaint was filed the victims' case was given an extraordinary boost by the discovery by Reed Brody and Olivier Bercault of HRW of an enormous cache of abandoned documents in the former DDS headquarters in N'Djamena. The two researchers had gone to the old DDS building near Chad's colonial-era cathedral, on a quiet backstreet facing the tree-lined banks of the Chari River, expecting just to get a feel for what had gone on there. In a dank back room covered with cobwebs, they stumbled over an untidy, foot-deep pile of documents. To their surprise and horror they found these documents detailed meticulously the fates of hundreds of prisoners, including death certificates, interrogation reports and identity cards. In one unearthed memo, the DDS director proudly affirmed that the DDS, 'thanks to the spider's web it has spun over the whole length of the national territory, keeps exceptional watch over the security of the State', as the 'eyes and ears of the President of the Republic, whose control it is under and to whom it reports on its activities'.[29] In total the documents revealed the names of 1208 people who were executed or who died in prison, as well as 12,321 victims of gross human rights violations. 'These documents were such great evidence of how widespread Habré's control had been. They would help us to determine the shape of the legal case in years to come', said Brody.

Next stop Belgium

The disappointment of the Senegalese case fresh in their minds, the next step in the fight for justice was when three Chadians who had become naturalised Belgian citizens filed a case in the Brussels district court, again taking advantage of the universal jurisdiction principle. Belgium was unique among European countries for having passed a law in 1993 permitting victims to file complaints in Belgium for atrocities committed abroad (although the Habré case was allowed to proceed, in 2003 the universal jurisdiction law was rescinded under pressure from the US and in particular Donald Rumsfeld, who had threatened Belgium that it risked losing its status as hosts to NATO's headquarters).[30] In early 2002 a Belgian investigating judge Daniel Fransen visited Chad along with a prosecutor to interview victims and former Habré henchmen, and to see mass graves and detention centres. The investigators took charge of the uncovered DDS documents, and a declaration in October that year from the Chadian authorities that Habré would not enjoy any form of immunity gave the victims' rights groups a renewed sense of optimism. A number of other victims filed additional complaints.

However, the Belgian case, like the Chadian and Senegalese efforts before it, was never able to fully take off and became entangled in a complex web of international legal wrangling and political interference. At first it proceeded at a glacial pace, taking four years of investigation by Judge Fransen before an arrest warrant was issued against Habré in 2005, charging him with crimes against humanity, war crimes, torture and serious violations of international humanitarian law. This was an important step forward and was followed quickly by the issuing of an extradition request by Belgium to Senegal and Habré's arrest two months later. But not long afterwards the Dakar Appeals court ruled that Senegal lacked jurisdiction to rule on the extradition request. A further three extradition requests from Belgium also led nowhere, with two of them being rejected on technical grounds because the legal papers submitted by the Senegalese government were not in order, suggesting that the Senegalese authorities were stalling or not taking the requests seriously.[31] A fourth and final request was sent in 2011, but was never answered. In frustration at the lack of action, Belgium took the case to the International Court of Justice (ICJ) in 2009, claiming that Senegal had breached its obligations under the UNCAT by failing to act to prosecute Habré, and by refusing to extradite him to Belgium for prosecution. The ICJ case was filed by Belgium on behalf of Chadian citizens and Belgian citizens of Chadian origin who claimed to be victims. The viewpoint that Senegal had failed in its obligations was shared by the UN Committee against Torture itself, which in 2006 had condemned Senegal for violating its obligations and called on the country to try the former president;[32] and in fact followed up the ruling with an unprecedented visit to Senegal in 2009.

The EAC: an African solution to an African problem?

While there was little progress on the efforts to extradite Habré to Belgium, there was by now some momentum building up behind the idea of holding a trial of Habré on African soil. In late 2005, in the midst of the flurry of legal cases filed against the former Chadian president, Senegal had referred the case of Habré to the AU, and with the support of Nigeria at its annual summit in January 2006 agreed to set up a 'Committee of Eminent African Jurists' to 'consider all aspects and implications of the Hissène Habré case as well as the options available for his trial'.[33] Six months later the body responded by requesting that Senegal should prosecute Habré 'on behalf of Africa', a sign perhaps that the body as a whole was keen to be seen to be 'combatting impunity'.[34] Somewhat surprisingly President Wade agreed. There were some encouraging signs, such as a new law passed in 2007 to allow the country to try crimes against humanity, war crimes and torture even when committed outside the country, and a constitutional amendment allowing cases to be tried retroactively.

applying to something in the past

However, this African-led initiative also came close to derailment on several occasions, again mostly due to Senegal's procrastinations. Firstly, Wade brought up the simple issue of money, claiming numerous times from 2008 to 2010 that Senegal could not afford the costs of the trial, which were initially estimated at €66 million ($79.2 million). This was eventually revised down to €8.6 million ($10.32 million), the funding of which was agreed at an international donor summit in 2010. But then came a challenge to Senegal's legal amendments from Habré's lawyers at the West African political grouping ECOWAS's regional court. It ruled in November 2010 just days before the donor's conference that Senegal could not try Habré without violating the *nullem crimen sine lege* principle which states that a person should not face criminal trial for an act which was not criminalised before the person performed the act. The ECOWAS court ruled therefore that Senegal's domestic courts were not competent to try Habré, but helpfully suggested that a tribunal of 'international character' could do so.

Under President Wade the ECOWAS ruling seemed to be the straw that broke the camel's back. In May 2011 Senegal unexpectedly withdrew completely from any further negotiations. Although the precise reasons are shrouded in mystery, the decision appears to be linked to the fears that an international tribunal would cost perhaps ten times what had been promised for the Senegalese court, and would pose enormous threats to Senegal's legal independence. 'Wade may have felt he was being dragged into something he just couldn't accept', speculates Reed Brody.[35]

The final blow came when Wade announced in July 2011 that Habré would be extradited to Chad within two days. The decision was condemned by the then UN Human Rights chief Navi Pillay, on the grounds that Habré had already been sentenced to death *in absentia* by a court in Chad in 2008 following a devastating rebel attack which he was accused of having supported, and that if sent back he would stand a realistic chance of torture and lack of a fair trial.[36] Eventually Wade reversed the decision, but then Chad seemed to wash its hands of the matter, requesting that the former president should be extradited to Belgium. This volte face was followed by another hopeless-seeming extradition request launched by Belgium. By the end of 2011 the situation was becoming almost farcical and the hopes of ever bringing Habré to trial looked very slim indeed. 'Between 2008 and 2011 I really started to lose hope', Clement Abaifouta later told me. 'When my family continued to be threatened I really thought about abandoning it. Abdoulaye Wade has left me with some really bad memories, he led us nowhere for eleven years.'[37]

The breakthrough

Although the odds looked stacked against them, the Chadian civil society campaigners and victims' groups never gave up hope. And in March 2012, the landscape shifted irrevocably. On 26 February, Senegal had held the first round of a presidential election with the ageing Abdoulaye Wade standing against a field of fourteen candidates. It had seemed that Wade was in a strong position – the country's Constitutional Court had just ruled that because he had assumed power in 2000 he was not bound by the terms of the country's 2001 Constitution which stipulated that presidents must be subject to a two-term limit. The decision had proved highly controversial, leading to street protests in the weeks leading up to the vote in which six people were killed.[38] However, in the second round of the elections, Wade faced former Prime Minister and president of the National Assembly, Macky Sall, who had vocally criticised the business dealings of Wade's unpopular son Karim Wade. It seems that ordinary Senegalese finally felt emboldened to reject Wade's ham-handed attempt to cling to power. Macky Sall won with around 65% of the vote and, to many people's surprise – neighbouring Mali had undergone a military coup unseating President Amadou Toumani Touré just a few days earlier – Wade conceded defeat. As jubilant supporters piled onto the streets of Dakar, Sall hailed 'a new era' for the country.

Hissène Habré was not the first person on everyone's mind as Senegal adjusted to life under its new leader. However the case was not unknown to the new president. Sall had in the past had some dealing with the Chadian victims' groups; Clement Abai-fouta had visited him on numerous occasions to appeal for his help, as had Abderahmane Gueye, a Senegalese businessman who was jailed in Habré's prisons during the 1980s along with his friend and Senegalese citizen Demba Gaye, who later died there.[39] Senegal's new Justice Minister, Aminata Touré (who would later become Senegal's Prime Minister), was a former women's rights campaigner who had also in the past expressed support for the idea of bringing Habré to trial. The victims' groups, assisted by HRW, saw their chance and swamped the new Senegalese authorities with requests for assistance. Within a few months, Sall had announced the formation of a working group to draw up the practicalities of organising a trial in Senegal, and on 15 July 2015 he announced at the AU summit in Addis Ababa that Habré would be tried.

The news came not a moment too soon, as just five days later the ruling in the long-running ICJ case launched by Belgium in 2009 finally landed. The ICJ ruling found that Senegal was in violation of its obligations under the UNCAT. The court also ruled that Senegal must either put Habré on trial 'without further delay' or comply with the Belgian requests to extradite him.[40] The ruling was greeted with joy by campaigners. It was also an embarrassment for Senegal's new leaders, hoping to project a new era and proud of their country's long-standing respect for human rights and its leadership in judicial matters and regard for the rule of law. Aminata Touré immediately confirmed that a trial would take place, and told the *New York Times* that 'we regret that for years this trial did not take place'.[41] Touré added that plans were already underway for a trial before Senegalese and African judges, in agreement with the African Union, which she called 'a novelty in international law'.

There has been some debate as to the extent to which the ICJ ruling was the decisive step which propelled Senegal into taking action to set up the EAC. As Konstatinos D. Magliveras argues, the judgment 'did not offer Senegal much room to manoeuvre'.[42] However, Reed Brody believes the real breakthrough was a political one. Despite Abdoulaye Wade's offers to expel Habré and his denunciations, including on more than one occasion calling him a criminal, he had still effectively blocked every initiative. It seems that Wade's concept of the principle of the brotherhood of African presidents – which he called the 'syndicat des chefs d'Etat' (Union of heads of state) – was more important to him than Senegal's reputation as a leader in justice. He simply could not abandon a former leader to the lions, but there was no doubt that the former Chadian president's presence on Senegalese soil gave him his fair share of headaches. When Wade went, the way had finally been cleared for a trial. 'The turning point was undoubtedly the election of Macky Sall', says Reed Brody.[43] It was now the AU's turn to demonstrate how it planned to deal with a serious case of historical human rights abuses.

Establishing the EAC: the first hybrid court in six years

Once the political hurdles had been removed, the EAC was finally established in August 2012 by Senegal and the African Union for the 'prosecution of international crimes committed on the territory of the Republic of Chad during the period from 7 June 1982 to 1 December 1990'.[44] Following the 2010 ECOWAS court ruling which had recommended a trial of 'international character', the EAC was established as a 'hybrid court'. Although there is no agreed definition of a hybrid court among academics, the 'hybridisation' comes from the fact that they incorporate a varying mix of international and national features – international and national staff and a compound of international and national substantial and procedural law. Hybrid courts are typically nationally run but internationally supported bodies, created to address particular situations and to sanction serious abuses of international law.

Hybrid trials were developed in the late 1990s as a response to the some of the criticisms levelled at the ICTY and ICTR. These institutions, although breaking important ground in prosecuting abuses, seemed to have done little to bolster the power of domestic courts and had been run by high-profile international legal teams without significant participation of local personnel. They were seen as distant to the people affected by the crimes. Hybrid courts also arrived at a very specific time in the development of international justice: 'the *interregnum,* the period between the adoption of the Rome Statute establishing the International Criminal Court (ICC) in 1998, and the coming into force of the court in 2002';[45] in effect they were perceived by many as a stop-gap before a permanent international institution took over. The fact that the ICC rested on a principle of 'complementarity' – that it would sit alongside domestic judicial systems and would only step in if they were incapable of trying domestic crimes – in theory suggested that trials which needed to blend international and national law would become obsolete with the passing of time.

The first hybrid courts were the creation of a SCSL in 2002 and the ECCC in 2004. Advocates believed that the hybrid model would deliver legitimacy without challenging domestic judicial sovereignty, that they would be quicker and cheaper than the big international trials, and that they would have a beneficial impact on domestic justice systems by virtue of the international elements of the courts rubbing shoulders with the national staff. These institutions did achieve a number of significant prosecutions such as those of Charles Taylor in Sierra Leone and Comrade Duch in Cambodia, and they were praised for the role they played in developing outreach so that justice could be understood by communities. However, as the years progressed, academics began to question if they 'entirely lived up to their promises'.[46] Dr Padraig McAuliffe, senior lecturer in law at University of Liverpool, has argued that they had 'fallen into practical obsolescence and theoretical disfavour'.[47] The hybrid courts of the early 2000s became plagued by accusations of political interference and lack of progress. For example, the ECCC set up to try Khmer Rouge-era human rights abuses became embroiled in criticisms of corruption and political interference from the Cambodian authorities, and the Sierra Leone court was criticised for having to try Charles Taylor in the Netherlands. The Special Court for Lebanon established to try those responsible for the murder of Rafik Hariri made slow progress. Academics have argued that rather than being designed in a systematic way, hybrid trials were actually pragmatic emergency responses to individual situations. This has meant that 'wider, more holistic rule of law development has been an afterthought at best'.[48]

The EAC was the first hybrid trial to be established since the Special Court for Lebanon in 2007. Its real novelty came from the fact that it was an *African hybrid court*; it was the first time that the courts of one African country were used to try the former leader of another African country under pan-African officials – presiding Judge Gustave Gberdao Kam was from Burkina Faso and the Chief Prosecutor Mbacké Fall was Senegalese. It was also the first time a universal jurisdiction case was able to proceed to trial in Africa. It was the first time the AU had independently set up a trial, and offered a chance to show that the regional body was serious and capable of tackling impunity.

There has been some academic debate as to the precise extent of the EAC's 'international hybrid' nature. The court only became hybrid because of the ECOWAS court decision which stipulated that only an 'international' tribunal could try Habré, a decision which has been questioned as a 'flawed finding' by a number of academics including Sarah Williams from the University of New South Wales. The EAC has been categorised as less of a pure hybrid trial, and 'at the limit of the category of internationalised criminal tribunals, and closer to situations in which national institutions received assistance, finance and training'.[49] The EAC participation has been described as 'minimal': there were only two trial judges, Gustave Gberdao Kam and Wafi Ouagadeye, who were not from Senegal. This is important as it raises the question of how much participation from international judges is desirable or politically acceptable. As we will see in the Conclusion, in general the more international staff are involved the more it is possible for detractors of any hybrid court to claim that domestic justice is being undermined.

The statute

The EAC's founding statute provides that it was to be established within the existing Senegalese justice system in order to 'prosecute and try the person(s) most responsible for crimes and serious violations of international law'.[50] Four 'chambers' were created: a Pre-Trial Chamber, an Indictment Chamber, a Trial Chamber and an Appeal Chamber, with jurisdiction to choose to prosecute the most serious crimes of genocide, crimes against humanity, war crimes and torture. The statute provided that former heads of state and government officials had no immunity from criminal responsibility (Article 10, 3). It also laid out the circumstances in which the accused could be convicted under the legal doctrine of 'command responsibility', where 'superiors can incur criminal liability for acts committed by their subordinates if they fail to prevent or punish subordinates for their unlawful actions'.[51] This legal principle was greatly developed by the ICTY and the ICC, which established that it did not have to be directly proved that the 'superior' had exact knowledge of every single act, rather it could be inferred or imputed that the 'superior' must have known or 'had reason to know that the subordinate was about to commit such acts or had done so' (Article 10, 4); in other words it is a form of responsibility for the omission to act',[52] or a failure to punish the acts of subordinates.

The statute laid out the principle of *Non bis in idem* (Article 19), the legal doctrine that no legal action can be instituted twice for the same cause of action, a point which was to become crucial concerning Habré's co-accused Saleh Younouss and Mahamat

Djibrine, who had been jailed in N'Djamena for their role in DDS torture in 2015. It also laid out the maximum penalties applicable to the crimes, an appeal process and provided that in the event of a conviction, reparations should be awarded to victims through the establishment of a Trust Fund made up of voluntary contributions from foreign governments and international organisations.

Significantly, it allowed for the forming of 'civil parties' with named lawyers to allow victims a greater role in the process. The principle of civil parties came into its own under the hybrid trials of the early 2000s, especially under the ECCC, which was set up to try the crimes of the Khmer Rouge. It allows victims and their lawyers to participate in trials in two stages: to assist in crafting the prosecution case and also during the trial when they are permitted to play a greater role than merely giving evidence, such as giving impact statements and suing for reparations. The 'civil parties' concept has been described as 'revolutionary'[53] as it turns on its head the idea – common in older styles of 'adversarial' trials – that the case must be decided between legal personnel with victims kept at a distance from the day-to-day proceedings of the court. For a time the idea of civil parties was promoted at the ICC, although in subsequent years the court has tried to limit the role of victims as it was seen as becoming unwieldy.

Finally the statute allowed for a significant campaign of outreach which was meant to ensure that the process was understood at the local level – practically this involved a sizeable budget for outreach activities and a commitment to filming the entire trial. The court's budget was to remain the €8.6 million ($10.32 million) promised at an international round table of donors in November 2010; commitments had already been made by Chad (US$3,743,000), the European Union (€2 million), the Netherlands (€1 million), the AU (US$1 million), the United States (US$1 million), Belgium (€500,000), Germany (€500,000), France (€300,000) and Luxembourg (€100,000).

Pre-trial phase

Once the statute and budget had been agreed, on 8 February 2013 the EAC was finally inaugurated by Ciré Aly Ba, the administrator of the new court. The pre-trial investigation phase by four Senegalese magistrates was launched and a trial was slated for early 2014. The early actions of the court demonstrated a seeming commitment to acting promptly. The Office of the Parquet General of the EAC visited Belgium in late May 2013 to discuss the case with Belgian prosecutors, to locate witnesses and help form their first submission.[54] A week later the team travelled to Chad for a week-long visit which included meeting the Chadian judiciary and victims' groups; the team also visited some of the sites of mass graves uncovered by the Chadian Commission of Enquiry and the former Habré-era detention centres.[55]

Things then moved very fast. On 30 June 2013 the unthinkable happened. Hissène Habré was arrested at his home in Ouakam, Dakar, by paramilitary police and taken to an unknown location.[56] Later that day the EAC announced at a press conference that he had been taken into Senegalese custody. On 2 July Habré was charged with war crimes, crimes against humanity and torture. The EAC also recommended the indictment of five Habré-era accomplices: Guihini Korei, Habré's nephew and former director of the DDS; Saleh Younouss, former director of the DDS; Mahamat Djibrine (El Djonto) one of the most feared torturers of the DDS; Abakar Torbo, former director of the DDS prison service; and Zakaria Berdei, a former security advisor at the presidency and one of those suspected of responsibility in the repression in the south in 1984.

Then, in a further shock move, thirteen Habré-era lieutenants including Saleh Younouss and Mahamat Djibrine were arrested in N'Djamena just a few days later, after twenty-three years of living freely. To many people's disbelief, Idriss Déby announced that Chad would cooperate with the Senegalese prosecutors, and even offered to testify himself. I was in Chad on the day of those arrests and attended a packed press conference held by Jacqueline Moudeina in a community centre, where hundreds of former victims and their families crammed into a small room, crying, singing and clapping their hands, desperate to hear what it all might mean. After so many failed attempts, some were still not entirely convinced that justice would ever be done[57] and there was still scepticism that the trial would be fair or impartial. Nevertheless, it really appeared that this time something was happening.

The indictments were followed by a series of four *'commissions rogatoires'* 'rogatory commissions' led by Chief Prosecutor Mbacke Fall which visited Chad between August 2013 and June 2014. The objective was to allow the EAC team to thoroughly develop their own investigation, based on the evidence already collected by the victims' groups, HRW and the Chadian Truth Commission. These missions were extraordinary in the level of detail collected: some 2500 'witnesses' and victims' statements and numerous interviews carried out with former Habré security agents. At the first hearing in a temporary office set up in N'Djamena's commissariat, an estimated 400 people claiming to be direct or indirect victims queued up outside to give testimony on the first day. An estimated 100 potential witnesses including some former DDS agents were interviewed at a second site. The EAC team tried to examine and make copies of the mountain of evidence collected from the DDS archives by Reed Brody and Olivier Bercault, which included an estimated 40,000 documents: 'It was almost impossible', says Henri Thulliez, a researcher for HRW who attended all four visits. 'It was a huge mess with practically a small hill of documents. There just wasn't enough time to look through everything.'[58] Some complained that their detailed testimonies had been reduced down to a few lines, or that they'd been asked to sign documents in French that they couldn't understand. During these four visits, experts appointed by the court also began their work, such as an Argentinian excavation team charged with digging up alleged sites of mass graves including the notorious 'Deli' site in southern Chad, a handwriting expert who was charged with trying to establish who had been responsible for the written orders, and a statistics expert who used information from the DDS archive to estimate the average death rate in Habré's jails. 'During those four visits we realised the mood had really changed', says Henri Thulliez. 'It was like people suddenly felt free to talk. Mbacké Fall [the Senegalese prosecutor] was serious and it was like suddenly people felt free to talk in a way they never had before.'[59]

On 13 February 2015 the EAC Pre-Trial Chamber announced following its investigations that there was sufficient evidence to proceed with a trial of Hissène Habré. A date was tentatively set for May or June that year. After more than twenty years of false starts, defiance and impossible legal entanglements, it really did appear that Hissène Habré was to get his day in court. Nevertheless, there had been little progress on the indictments of the other five co-accused. According to Reed Brody, the last confirmed sighting of Guihini Korei had been in Benin at the time of Habré's arrest, although writer Jerome Tubiana claims that he was known to be in southern Libya in early 2017;[60] no one seemed to know where Abakar Torbo Rahama was; and Zakaria Berdei was believed to have been living in secure hiding in Chad for many years.

The N'Djamena trial

The cases of Saleh Younouss and Mahamat Djibrine – having been arrested in Chad in July 2013 – were more complicated. In November 2014, just six months before the EAC was due to open its doors, the decision was made that they would be tried in Chad itself, apparently in defiance of the EAC arrest warrants which aimed to secure their extradition to Dakar. Younouss and Djibrine went on trial along with around twenty other former DDS agents who had been arrested in July 2013, accused of murder, torture, kidnapping, arbitrary detention, and assault and battery. The case provoked a storm in Chad, being the first time any DDS figures had publicly spoken. So many people turned out to witness the trial that it had to be moved from N'Djamena's Palais de Justice to the former seat of the National Assembly. Over two months, around fifty victims testified in a jam-packed court, creating great drama as some of the agents had refused to speak and others had tried to implicate their co-accused in angry exchanges across the courtroom. Saleh Younouss repeatedly pleaded his innocence, saying that simply being the director of the DDS was not a crime in itself. All categorically denied their own involvement in the charges of murder, torture and kidnapping. At times the judge was forced to cut off members of the DDS who tried to vociferously defend themselves. Highlights of the case were shown every night on Chadian TV and were avidly followed by many.

On 25 March 2015, twenty of the accused were convicted, including Younouss and Djibrine, who were both sentenced to life with hard labour. Others convicted include Nodjigoto Haunan, former director of the National Security Agency, implicated in the repression against the Zaghawa ethnic group, and Khalil Djibrine, former department head of the DDS in the south of Chad during the repression there of 1983–84.[61] Lesser sentences ranged from five to twenty years.[62] Three people were acquitted, including the last director of the DDS in 1990, Toke Dady. The court president also decided that the Chadian state was liable for half of the damages awarded to the 7000 registered victims, which were set at 75 billion CFCA ($125 million) and ordered that a museum and memorial commemorating the victims should be built. Lawyers for the civil parties and victims reacted with delight to the convictions: 'I feel so light, it's like a burden has been lifted from my shoulders', victim Fatimeh told the *Justice Tribune* magazine.[63]

It was a remarkable development, a trial which had been avoided for more than twenty years by the Chadian authorities. Jean-Bernard Padaré, a prominent Chadian lawyer and Minister of Justice at the time of the establishment of the EAC, told me that the case had been made possible because finally the way had been cleared 'at the highest political level'. It was a hugely significant move for Chad which had for so many years shied away from confronting its past. Victims' groups were jubilant: 'Finally, finally, the men who brutalized us and then laughed in our faces for decades have got their comeuppance', said Clément Abaifouta after they were jailed.[64]

However, the conclusion of the case created new judicial headaches. Although the EAC claimed that as an internationalised trial it should have precedence over Chad's domestic courts, it seemed now all but impossible to transfer Younouss and Djibrine to Senegal for the opening of the case against Habré and his five co-accused. It was never clearly established that the EAC had jurisdiction to try them, seeing as one of the reasons Senegal was allowed to try Habré was because he resided there,[65] and at the same time the EAC statute did not allow individuals to be tried again for a crime of which they had already been convicted. In addition, Chad also refused to transfer the prisoners and even turned down a request to let them testify by video link just a month before the DDS trial began in November 2014.

Former Minister of Justice Jean-Bernard Padaré suggests that there was a feeling that political elites in Chad did not want the case to go any further than the N'Djamena DDS trial: 'I was in Dakar ready to sign an agreement that would have allowed for the transfer of the prisoners to the EAC, I had even called a press conference and journalists were waiting for the story', he says. 'But at the last minute I received a call from the highest levels saying that I had to cancel the announcement. I had to quickly invent another reason for holding the press conference.'[66] His story chimes with the perception from some quarters that as the momentum built towards the opening of the EAC, Chadian authorities were beginning to panic. The formerly cooperative relationship between Chad and the EAC appeared to be becoming strained. 'The N'Djamena trial did seem rushed and not that well-prepared', says Reed Brody. 'I suspect the trial was brought forward so as to avoid the extradition requests and therefore to prevent the danger of any former DDS agents saying too much.'[67] This problem was to continue throughout the EAC trial itself, where the issue of the responsibility of others besides Habré continued to be raised.

Chapter 3

THE EXTRAORDINARY AFRICAN CHAMBERS

On 19 July 2015 I packed my bags and set off on overnight flights from London via Morocco to Dakar, Senegal. As a freelance journalist it's always difficult making the decision to book expensive flights and hotels and to leave a young family behind. Who's really interested in this story? Will I get enough commissions to cover my costs? And after ten years' experience of covering African legal processes as part of the daily news grind, what's the chance that the trial will open for an hour, there will be some complex legal argument and the case will be adjourned for two months? Can I afford to take this risk? But after eight years of reporting on Chad, which had included many stories on the minutiae of the convoluted attempts to bring Habré to justice, I felt compelled to be there.

HRW's Reed Brody had strongly encouraged me to come in the days before the trial opened, but as the plane took off into the dark sky above Casablanca, four hours delayed and just three hours before the court was due to open, I was still nervous the rumours that Habré was planning not to show up for the trial would turn out to be true. My fears were partially assuaged when I arrived sleep-deprived the next morning at the imposing gates of the Palais de Justice in downtown Dakar, a stone's throw from the sea and the Cap Manuel maison d'arrêt where Habré had spent the last two years incarcerated; hordes of journalists, camera crews and former colleagues were packed up against the gates – evidently they were all expecting something to happen. Smiling Senegalese policemen were checking identity cards and ushered a number of reporters through, including me, although I had not yet secured accreditation for the court proceedings. It seemed a relaxed and open process.

Inside the building, crowds of civil society activists and Senegalese lawyers were milling around, sipping coffee from paper cups. We passed our bags through an airport scanner, and moved swiftly into the impressive main courtroom to escape the stifling humidity outside. Around five different camera crews were setting up equipment on all sides of the room, flash-lights popping and wires trailing across the floor. A large section of seating on the left was marked 'Press' but the gathered press corps were too excited to sit down. Across the floor I spotted Jacqueline Moudeina, elegant as ever in her legal robes, throngs of reporters pushing microphones into her face. A few metres away, Clement Abaifouta was chatting to the team from HRW. A strikingly tall, gaunt man in legal robes, with a carefree afro and goofy teeth was pacing along the bench at the front of the room, looking intense. 'Who's that?' I whispered to a Chadian journalist who had travelled to Dakar with financial help from the EAC's Outreach Consortium, which was charged with ensuring the trial got the maximum amount of publicity in Chad itself.

'That's Ciré Cledor Ly, he used to be Habré's lawyer. But I think he sacked him' … 'Ah bon?' Confused I scanned the room, fretful that I might manage to not notice the arrival of the day's most wanted man. 'Where will Habré be?' 'Over there', said the Chadian journalist. At the front of the room, there was a single black leather armchair opposite the judges' bench. Two burly Senegalese security agents stood with their arms crossed, staring unflinchingly into the distance. On the other side of the room a commotion broke out. I spotted one of Chad's most famous sons, the film director Mahamat-Saleh Haroun, dressed in a crisp white shirt and sunglasses, waving his arms at a court official. 'What's going on?', I whispered to my

Chadian colleague. 'He wants to film, he's making a documentary. But the court said we're only allowed to use the footage from the official court feed; after this opening session all other cameras will be banned.' My heart sank and along with it some half-hearted plans to make my own TV documentary about the case. Eighteen months later I did in fact see Haroun's final product, a beautiful but sobering documentary profiling Habré's victims, entitled *Hissène Habré: A Chadian Tragedy*. To the EAC's credit, even the great man himself – now Chad's Minister of Culture – had been unable to persuade them to let him film any of the proceedings.

An hour later, we were all still there. The room was getting hot and the reporters had appeared to run out of questions. A few people sat in chairs and fanned their faces with notepads. Others milled in and out, drinking more coffee. I started to wonder if this had all been a monumental waste of time.

Then suddenly a scuffle broke out in the corner of the room. The assembled horde leapt to its feet, camera-phones at the ready. The TV crews raced across the floor, trailing wires and sound-men behind them. I stood on tiptoes to see what was happening.

'Il est là!' someone shouted. Where? I couldn't see him. I felt stupid and waved my smartphone in the general direction of the cacophony.

And then I worked it out. He was right in the middle of the commotion. A flash of white and I just about made out his pristine, perfectly folded head-to-toe 'boubou'. His head was wrapped in a white scarf to just above his nose, and he was wearing gold-rimmed dark glasses. At seventy-two, he still had something of the baby-faced dictator about him. His stance was limp like a rag doll, as he was being pushed from side to side by the Senegalese security agents. Several people – his supporters I presumed – shoved their way toward the front of the court shouting histrionically. For a few seconds I just stood and stared. After all these years of chasing this story – nothing, compared to the twenty-five years Clement Abaifouta and Souleymane Guengueng had been battling for justice – it was hard to believe that I was actually getting a glimpse of Hissène Habré.[1]

Habré held his fist up to cheers from the supporters, people were jumping over chairs to reach him. He began shouting. I could only pick out of a few words over the racket, 'colonialists', 'traitors'. A later transcript of a recording of the brouhaha revealed he had shouted 'Down with imperialists. [The trial] is a farce by rotten Senegalese politicians. African traitors. Valet of America'.[2] The Senegalese security agents were looking concerned and tried to push him down into the leather chair. I glanced behind me to see Jacqueline, Clement, Souleymane and the HRW team looking on with glassy stares. Eventually the Senegalese agents got the order to remove Habré from the room. Slowly but surely they pushed him through the crowd, his supporters desperately trying to grab him. All the time he seemed to drag his heels and curl his shoulders inwards – perhaps to convey submission but I suspect more likely to give the impression of a victimised, feeble old man. As he reached the gate to the cells, he held up his arm in a triumphant gesture and I noticed a clutch of gris-gris beads in his fist. The supporters gave one final rousing cheer, clapping their hands wildly as the man who had once shaken Reagan's hand was picked up by the legs in the most undignified manner and hauled over the gate to the cells by the Senegalese security agents. He disappeared from view.

After ten more minutes of shouting and chaos as Habré's supporters tried to break through the row of police, the most disruptive supporters were removed by Senegalese police and the court was summoned. The judges of the EAC made their entrance. At the centre, dressed in red, white and black robes, was Gustave Gberdao Kam, a Burkinabe selected as the EAC Trial Chamber's presiding judge. Close by was Chief Prosecutor Mbacké Fall. Kam calmly asked the court to be seated. The adrenaline was still pumping through the air as the unflappable Kam began a remarkably calm speech in which he announced the opening of the court and the decision to adjourn until the following day to see if Habré would attend. And with that we were all dismissed. After posting off a few frantic dispatches about the courtroom drama to the *Guardian*, I spent the rest of the day hanging out at the hotel where Reed Brody and most of the Chadian civil society campaigners were based. No one was sure what it would mean, what they should do. Would it indeed turn out to be an adjournment?

The next morning was much calmer. The court was remarkably prompt and well-organised and this time Judge Kam had the foresight to make sure that Habré had been delivered without fanfare to his leather armchair before anyone else arrived. A glimpse of gleaming white was just barely visible behind the phalanx of black-clothed, masked Senegalese security men. I glanced over at Souleymane Guengueng who was perched on the packed civil parties' bench next to Reed Brody; Guengueng was quietly crying and Reed had his arm around his shoulder.

Journalists were ordered to sit, cameras were barred. Kam seemed determined to keep proceedings on track. However, this session again did not last long. Judge Kam made several attempts to address Habré, who remained defiantly silent. Although Maitre François Serres, Habré's official French lawyer, was sitting at the back of the hall, he also refused to address the court to represent Habré. Serres later told *Le Monde* that his strategy was 'a defence of refusal',[3] and continued Habré's line about the EAC being an illegitimate court, a politically motivated 'farce' in which Habré was a 'scapegoat'. The decision to remain silent seemed a high-risk strategy which would likely result in Habré's unquestioned conviction, but Habré again said nothing and didn't react when Judge Kam informed him that the court would now adjourn for forty-five days to allow a court-appointed defence team to prepare to represent him. The team would be made up of Maitres Mbaye Sène, Abdou Gning and Mounir Ballal, all from the Dakar bar. Judge Kam's decision was followed by a series of eloquent and impassioned speeches by seasoned European lawyers who had flown in to represent the Chadian civil society parties, such as

the Frenchman William Bourdon and the Belgian Georges-Henri
Beauthier, who said that the forty-five-day adjournment risked
'flouting justice again'.

Kam listened patiently, but then continued with his decision
to dismiss the court. Another ugly scene broke out, with pushing
and shoving between groups of Habré supporters and some of the
victims. As Habré was again lifted high above the imbroglio by the
Senegalese security agents, keeping up the act as a perfectly poised
martyred mummy in his white robes, the supporter began chanting
and clapping their hands. When he reached the gates to the cells
 and was pushed over he held up his hand in a V for Victory salute,
which sent the crowd into raptures. It was a remarkably shocking
gesture to the victims and their legal representatives who sat quietly
on the other side of the room. Some of them began to leave. Jacqueline Moudeina pushed past me, I ran after her chasing a comment.
'Jacqueline has left the building', she told me gruffly, holding her
hand up to signal she did not want to talk. All around me the corre-
spondents were hacking away at smartphones, searching for a quiet
corner to do a telephone interview with their stations.

In fact once the chaos had died down, the victims' groups were
remarkably phlegmatic about the delay. They felt it was insignificant,
and important in the name of justice that he should get a defence
team and a fair trial. Many of them were simply overwhelmed by
the fact of having seen Habré in court, powerless and unable to
dictate to anyone. 'I experienced a profound emotion when I saw
him there', Clement Abaifouta told me immediately after the court
closed, seeming still in shock. 'All of the pain and hurt I experienced
came back to me. But after twenty-five years to see someone who
hurt you in that position. It has changed everything. It's like I am in
the sun and he is in the shade'.[4]

'Even if the delay is for another two or three months,
that's not more than the twenty-five years we've already been
waiting for justice', Souleymane Guengueng told me. 'During
his rule he was like a god. Everyone was scared of him. No one

could believe that this man who used to be like a god could so easily be judged'.[5]

That evening, I managed to grab a few quiet moments with Reed Brody at the Hotel Sokhamon on the Dakar peninsula sea front. We drank a beer and looked out into the black above the gently rolling Atlantic washing against the shore. He was also sanguine about the delay and Habré's attempt to challenge the legitimacy of the court. 'How ironic, how can he say the court is full of imperialists? He was the one who was supported by the US and France during his rule and it was the Chadian victims who were instrumental in setting this up. All the judges are African!', he said. He felt the EAC had resolutely shown their commitment to continue. 'All over Africa it is the victims who will understand that they have the power to give people hope.'[6]

When the case reopened on 7 September 2015, there was more palpable excitement that Habré would again succeed in disrupting events. Not one for disappointing, the former president again refused to leave his cell. Again Judge Kam had to order his appearance by force, and he was carried into the room in a similarly martyr-like fashion (and perhaps a touch of irony) by his by-now-familiar Senegalese security agents. For the first few hours he continued to make a scene, struggling with the guards and shouting 'Shut up! Shut up!' at a court clerk who was reading a list of charges and the names of some of his alleged victims. Once again his supporters cheered and clapped in support. However Judge Kam was not to be deterred from his mission and after several sharp warnings to the assembled room that disruptive behaviour would not be accepted and disruptors would be charged with contempt of court, he pushed the proceedings forward. Despite the fact that the three Senegalese lawyers appointed by the court to mount his defence explained that Habré had refused to talk to them at all in the forty-five days since the last adjournment, Judge Kam ordered that the case would nevertheless proceed.[7] From this point onwards the histrionics stopped. Habré, in his black leather armchair, settled into a smouldering silence which to this day has never been broken.

The court prepared itself for three months of compelling testimony of the gruesome and harrowing events which took place in the DDS prisons from 1982 to 1990.

The case

The evidence

The first few days of the evidence were something of a warming up. The court was given a historical perspective on Habré's rule by an independent Chadian historian, Arnaud Djingammadji, who was one of the only witnesses in the entire ninety-day testimony phase who mentioned the US and French support of Habré during the 1980s. Witnesses were called to give a view of the former president's character and background, including opposition figure and former Prime Minister under Idriss Déby, Jean Bawoyeu Alingué. Together they created the impression of an effective administrator, but a distant and cool character who mostly did not deign to talk to them. Alingué stressed that he found it difficult to imagine that Habré had been unaware of what was going on.

On day seven Mike Dottridge began his testimony in his capacity as a researcher on Central Africa for Amnesty International from 1979 to 1986 and later Africa programme head (although the Chad brief had fallen to his colleague Steven Ellis, who unfortunately died a few years before the trial started). A record of the court proceedings describes his testimony as 'marked by its impeccable rigour'.[8] The evidence he provided – including the reports of the execution of ninety Codos rebels and fifty-one people disappeared from the south during Black September in 1984 – appears to have impressed the court with the attention to fact-checking and detail. 'Most of the evidence we gathered was from Chadian exiles who arrived in Paris and we were scrupulous in cross-checking facts. We were trying to understand and build up the right picture, and not to just repeat anything we heard', Dottridge later told me in a London pub on a dark December evening.[9]

In court, Dottridge talked eloquently about women being used as sexual slaves and the shock of seeing 'veritable skeletons' walking out of the DDS jails in the early 1990s when the Amnesty team was permitted by President Déby to continue its research in the country; these images reminded him of 'the Second World War'. He added that many people had died in the prisons not as a direct consequence of torture, but of poor diet and withheld medical care. In his resumé of the evidence gathered throughout the 1980s he mentioned a number of torture methods such as the 'baguettes' and *'arbatachar'*, as well as the growing evidence of disappearances, extrajudicial killings and exactions on local populations by Chadian troops. Dottridge described the campaigning methods Amnesty used during the 1980s, which principally involved sending protest cards about individual cases of human rights abuses through membership networks. Amnesty researchers also carried out a number of media interviews where concerns about Chad were raised and a number of specific appeals were launched, including in 1987 when Amnesty called for the liberation of prisoners of conscience and an enquiry into prison deaths.

Dottridge was subjected to a detailed cross-examination by the court-appointed defence team. The questions focused on why Amnesty had not immediately addressed their concerns to the president, to which the Amnesty researcher cited a number of correspondences they had sent to the presidency, and also messages they had sent to Goukouni Oueddei when he was president of Chad in the early 1980s. Dottridge confirmed that the team had made only one visit to Chad during Habré's rule, in 1985, when they were supposed to meet directly with the president but the meeting was cancelled at the last moment apparently because the Congolese president was visiting. Defence lawyer Mounir Ballal tried to pursue the line that Amnesty had lacked independence and seemed to suggest a conspiracy between HRW, Amnesty and the 1992 Truth Commission; he asked on several occasions if there was a 'similitude' between the reports of the Truth Commission and Amnesty's

1980s short briefings. He appeared to suggest that Amnesty and the president of the commission, Mahamat Hassan Abakar, had been working together 'in a narrow fashion',[10] and quoted a US Secretary of State as saying that Amnesty supported US foreign policy; nonetheless there had been a long history of US support for Habré during the 1980s. Dottridge told the court that he had indeed met the Commission president during a visit in 1991 when they had discussed human rights abuses in the 1980s, but had subsequently lost contact with him. He told the court that his relationship with Reed Brody had been little more than a chance meeting in Brussels years after he had stopped working for Amnesty in 1995. 'He [Ballal] certainly needed access to more accurate information regarding Amnesty's policies and practices in the years pre-1991', Dottridge told me after the trial.[11]

The Amnesty evidence was followed by a gruelling three-day presentation by the former president of the Chadian Truth Commission, Mahamat Hassan Abakar. He explained how the commission had gone about its work, uncovering mass graves and interviewing ex-victims, and detailing what they had found out about the cases of torture and human rights abuses in jails. He explained how they had arrived at the figure of 40,000 deaths, and his presentation was accompanied by a film made by the Commission which showed bones and skulls sticking out of the ground at the site of one of the mass graves. When questioned on Habré's direct responsibility for what went on in the DDS jails, Abakar told the court that Saleh Younouss, a former director of the DDS, had confirmed to him that it was the former president himself who chose the directors of the service, and who had transformed the agency into 'an instrument of terror'.[12] Abakar gave details of claims of direct orders from the president to execute people, and vouched for the authenticity of some of the documents uncovered by HRW.

There was high drama as Abakar's testimony was interrupted by a heckler, a nephew of Habré, Mahamat Togoi, who stood up and shouted 'Liar, traitor!' as he was speaking. True to his word about keeping the court process on track, Judge Kam promptly sentenced Togoi to five months in prison for contempt of court. Abakar was then subjected to a barrage of questions from Habré's defence lawyers. They claimed that he had been too close to President Déby, that his language was partial and that the report had only been written as a political tool to discredit Habré. They asked why he hadn't pushed for the recommendations in his report to be implemented, to which he replied that he wasn't a 'superman' and given the political climate at the time in Chad he had not had the energy for the fight. 'Back in 1992 I didn't expect anything to come of the report .... We soon saw that Déby began using the same methods as Habré', Abakar later told me during an interview in Chad, eight months after the verdict. The defence lawyers also challenged his use of the figure of 40,000 deaths (calculated by assuming that the Commission had only spoken to 10% of victims) as unreliable. 'I stand by that figure. No-one kept a list but I am absolutely sure we have consistently underestimated the figure', said Abakar during my interview. 'The cross-examination by the defence lawyers was tiring. I understand that he wasn't collaborating, and they had to do something. But their strategy appeared to be nothing more than denigrating everything I said.'[13]

Next up was the Belgian investigator Daniel Fransen, who had carried out an investigating visit to Chad following the deposition of the universal jurisdiction case in Belgium by a group of Chadian victims. Fransen explained to the court in greater detail how he and his team had worked in Chad, visiting the sites of mass graves and taking witness statements. His testimony was followed by the statistics expert Patrick Ball, who had accompanied the EAC investigating team to Chad in 2013. His job had been to calculate the average rate of mortality in DDS prisons during the 1980s, based on the seized DDS documents. He told the court that the mortality rate had been between 90 and 400% higher than would normally be expected in the Chadian population, with an average daily death rate of 0.6% per 100 detainees. On one day – 23 June 1988 – it had peaked at 2.37 deaths per 100 detainees. He compared the death rates to those experienced in the Second World War by US soldiers at the hands of Japanese and Germans captured by the Russians.[14]

However, the real drama began when a former DDS agent Bandjim Bandoum took the stand – the only witness from 'inside' who was to testify against the former leader in front of the EAC after Chad had barred the extradition of other close accomplices, most of whom had been jailed in N'Djamena in 2015. Bandoum had joined the armed wing of the DDS in 1982 and had played a complex role negotiating with and reportedly betraying a group of southern rebels. He had been singled out by the 1991 Commission of Enquiry as one of the agency's fourteen most 'pitiless' torturers. Following several years of directing torture and interrogation, Bandoum claimed to have suffered a mental breakdown, and when he tried to flee Chad he had found himself in a DDS prison. Eventually released and allowed to return to work, he claimed his prison experience had convinced him to expose the truth about the oppressive system. He began passing information to contacts in the French military and eventually the French spirited him out of Chad, from where he began a long and difficult period of exile in Paris.[15]

Taking the stand, Bandoum, an imposing thick-set man, talked about conditions in 'Cellule C', where prisoners were crowded in and often had to drink their own urine to quench their thirst. He talked about the case of Rose Lokissim, a young woman who had been caught smuggling documents to Codos rebels and been thrown into a DDS prison. The last day of her life was poignantly captured in the documents uncovered by HRW, which revealed that during her final interrogation when she had been accused of smuggling messages to relatives about conditions in the prisons, DDS agents had found her to be 'irredeemable'. She had said then that even if she died, Chad would one day thank her. Bandoum told the Chambers that her file had been marked 'E' for execution. Bandoum confirmed that torture was systematically practised by the armed wing of the DDS, the BSIR, but claimed that he

FORMER DDS AGENT

heroism uncovered

personally had never tortured or killed anyone. He talked vividly of 'razzias' or raids on villages where DDS and BSIR agents had confiscated property and chased people from their homes, and chillingly about the way corpses were disposed of in the dead of night; he claimed that there were other mass graves which the EAC was unaware of. He talked about a special commission which was set up in 1987 to target the Hadjerai community. Bandoum's evidence on the complicity of Habré was also important: he claimed to have seen the former president at least once in the DDS headquarters, and he was sure that individual case files he had handled had been passed on to the president for approval and came back marked with 'E' for execution, 'L' for freedom (liberation) and 'V' for seen ('vu'). At the end of what was surely a difficult session for the victims who had been forced to listen to the former DDS agent, Bandoum called on Habré, who was sitting just a few metres from him, to address the court in order to help Chad 'turn the page'.[16] He also asked for the forgiveness of the victims, adding that he knew 'a pardon is not enough'.

The next stage of the trial examined the repression against the Hadjerai and Zaghawa communities in the later part of Habré's rule. The court heard from a number of witnesses who recounted harrowing stories of disappearances of family members from whom no word has ever been heard, and torture methods such as 'arbatachar' and forced drinking of water in DDS jails. Chief among these witnesses was Zakaria Fadoul Kitir, a retired university professor and representative of another victims' association. He was arrested after agreeing to help a student to correct an essay, his crime appearing to be being a Zaghawa with links to Idriss Déby. He described terrible conditions in jail, and the fact that he lost seven of his brothers and half-brothers and sisters in the pogrom against the Zaghawa community. The court also heard from Mahamat Nour Dadji, the son of Ahmat Dadji, a Hadjerai political leader who had been seized at his home at midnight by Habré's nephew Guihini Korei and one of the most feared torturers of the DDS, Mahamat Djibrine (El Djonto). At the end of his testimony he turned directly to Habré and asked him why the DDS had not been able to establish his father's guilt before he was killed. There was no response from the former president beyond a slight twitching of his feet. The wife of prominent Hadjerai journalist Saleh Ngaba, who had worked for several international media and whose story had been widely shared by Amnesty International as a 'prisoner of conscience', gave testimony about his disappearance. The court heard how Hassan Djamous – the commander of the Chadian army who would go on to become a hero of the anti-Habré struggle – had arrived in the town of Bitkine in Guera region, the Hadjerai homeland, and presided over the arrest of teachers, journalists and nurses, some of whom were tortured and later executed, while others were transferred by military plane to N'Djamena. More tales followed of people forced to dig mass graves or prepare food for thousands of emaciated prisoners and executions of groups of fifteen or more prisoners in the bush. Mariam Hassan Bagueri told the court about the disappearance of her husband, a prominent Hadjerai businessman who had previously sold vehicles to the presidency; she claimed in court that she had been told Habré had personally strangled her husband. Again the former president refused to answer when this accusation was put to him.[17] As the court followed the development of the 1989 Zaghawa rebellion against Habré, led by Idriss Déby and Hassan Djamous, Oumar Déby Itno, the younger brother of the current president, gave testimony. He described how in the days after Djamous and Déby had launched their rebellion, carloads of soldiers had arrived at their house and seized a number of his brothers and cousins, some of whom were later killed. He had only escaped by jumping over a wall and hiding in a neighbour's house for two days; he had then fled the town.

The testimony concerning the fate of the Hadjerais was followed by an unnerving session with the team of six Argentinian investigators who had travelled to Chad during the EAC's preparatory mission in 2013 to dig up and examine a number of the sites of mass graves. The most notorious of these sites was the so-called 'Deli farm' grave near Moundou in Logone Occidentale province. In 1984, at the beginning of Black September about 500 combatants from the Codos rebel groups had been called to this enormous state-owned farm site to discuss reconciliation and plans for disarmament and reintegration into the Chadian army. They stayed there for several weeks taking part in military exercises and handing over their weapons. Apparently tricked into believing that they were to take part in a reintegration ceremony which would allow them to join the national army, at least 200 of the Codos fighters had gathered unarmed in the fields early one morning only to be gunned down in a surprise attack by elements of the FANT.[18] Numerous employees at the farm and local people who came to see what had happened were also killed as the army moved through the site. According to the HRW report 'Plaine des Mortes',[19] local people claimed to have buried 203 that day. The Argentinian excavating team told the EAC that they had uncovered twenty-one bodies, most of them killed by gunshot, and several of whom had their hands tied behind their backs. Others showed signs of having been attacked before being killed. The team also confirmed they had found more skeletons in graves at Koumra and Gadjira, also in the south, some of which appeared to have been killed by gunshot. The Argentinian team confirmed that not all of the site at Deli Farm had been excavated.

The Deli massacre was part of the events of the so-called Black September the wave of repression against rebel groups in the country's south that began in 1984, which was further examined by the court. Eight witnesses described horrific attacks on villages and seemingly endless tales of repression, torture, killings and disappearances. The court heard from Mallah Ngabouli, a sugar trader who was accused of giving money to the Codos rebels. He was arrested with around fifteen other prisoners, most of whom were executed. DDS agents tied him by the neck to the back of a vehicle

EXCAVATORS

and dragged him through the bush; he sustained a broken jaw, broken teeth and a dislocated shoulder. He was transferred to the Camp des Martyrs where he was kept in a cell with a dead body for two weeks. It was another three years before he was released, when he claimed to have met President Habré, who told him not to bear any grudges. Another witness described sustained attacks on the village of Koumra, which the then Minister of the Interior, Brahim Itno, had described as overrun with Codos sympathisers. Moutedé Djim Hyngar told the court of a number of massacres of young men, showing the court his meticulously prepared list of those who had died. A particularly compelling witness was Hissein Robert Gambier, who also appeared in Mahamat-Saleh Haroun's aforementioned moving film. Gambier, whose father was French, described how he had spent five years in a DDS jail because of his light skin, which meant that he was accused of being a Libyan. Frequently breaking down and shaking with emotion, Gambier, who lost most of his hearing after he was subject to the 'baguette' punishment, and suffered sexual dysfunction after being hung by the testicles, claimed to have counted 2053 deaths during his incarceration. He earned the sobriquet 'the man who runs faster than death' for surviving five years in prison.

The court also heard from a number of former northern rebels and prisoners of war who had been captured during the fighting between Goukouni Oueddei's FAP and the FANT in the earlier part of Habré's rule. Idriss Abdoulaye described how he had been taken prisoner after a FAP attack on the village of Kalait. He was tied up with a group of his co-detainees who were shot by FANT soldiers; he was the only survivor. Ousmane Abakar was a teenager when he joined the ranks of the FAP just before the lightning offensive against Habré's base at Faya Largeau in 1983. In the brutal counter-offensive by the FANT he was taken prisoner and along with over 1000 others was transferred to a camp close to N'Djamena. Abakar talked about the appalling conditions in jail, where his hands and feet swelled up because of malnutrition and prisoners around him died from simple problems such as diarrhoea because there was no medication. Abakar described how one day in August 1983 he had witnessed at least 150 detainees, mostly Chadian Arabs and Gorane Kredas, being taken out to be 'executed'. These detainees were driven a short distance away to the village of Ambing where they were killed, a notorious massacre which was recounted to the 1992 Truth Commission by the sole survivor, Bichara Djibrine Ahmat. Prisoners were put into groups of fifty, tied together and gunned down by DDS agents, reportedly in front of Guihini Korei and Abakar Torbo. The bodies were left out in the open for several months before they were hastily buried by the army. The site of the mass grave was uncovered and excavated by the Truth Commission, whose evidence was available to the EAC. Bichara Djibrine Ahmat, who testified before the EAC that he had seen Hissène Habré on the battlefield at Faya Largeau, gave the following account to Mahamat Hassan Abakar's researchers in 1991:

> They took us to a place which was surrounded with spiky small bushes. The soldiers lined up in a semi-circle around us and opened fire without the least concern for our screams and cries. We cried and begged so loud that the people from local villages would have heard us if the cries hadn't been covered by the sound of the guns. Eventually the screams subsided but the shooting continued until no one was moving anymore.

Many of these prisoners of war were kept in jail throughout Habré's rule – in Ousmane Abakar's case for four and a half years – although many more joined their ranks after the devastating FANT attack on the Libyan air base at Ouadi Doum in 1987. During this time only very rare visits of the International Committee of the Red Cross were permitted to just one prison in N'Djamena,[20] and many of the prisoners were effectively hidden from the agency in contravention of international law. Only fifty-three of the Libyan POWs taken during the long years of fighting in the 1980s were ever registered with the organisation.[21] Ousmane Abakar and others were finally released into the custody of the ICRC in 1987, where they were given badly needed medical care and nutritious food.

Sexual violence as a war crime

If the harrowing evidence of torture, disappearances and arbitrary killings was not already difficult enough for the assembled courtroom to hear, starting on 19 October the court was electrified by the testimony of four women who were sent in 1988 with five other women to the Ouadi Doum military base, approximately 100 kilometres north-east of Faya Largeau in the desert wastelands of Ennedi province – the base which Habré's forces had dramatically overrun in 1987 forcing Libya into a humiliating retreat. Here the women, Khadidja Hassan Zidane, Khaltouma Déffallah, Houawa Birahim Faraj (who was just thirteen at the time of her arrest) and Hadjé Mérami Ali, were forced to cook and fetch water for a group of Chadian soldiers guarding the prized base. In the evenings they were subject to repeated sexual assaults and were effectively treated as sex slaves. The four women bravely stood in front of the court and gave their testimony. Khaltouma Deffallah, an air hostess with Air Afrique, had been arrested on a brief stop-over at N'Djamena airport by the DDS agent Abakar Torbo. She told the court how she had left her eight-year-old daughter with her domestic helper in Abidjan and was to spend more than a year trapped in Ouadi Doum without being able to contact her. Her voice shaking she told the court how in the evening the women had been used as sexual slaves, but then expressed her pride at being able to testify in front of the court after so many years. Hadjé Mérami Ali, arrested after a trip to Libya and accused of supplying documents to Libyans, sobbed as she described how her twelve-year-old daughter had died as a result of the sexual violence she was subjected to.

Standing alone in the witness box in the full glare of the television cameras and the gaze of the entire courtroom made up of Habré's supporters, journalists and almost exclusively male judges and officials, Houawa Birahim Faraj struggled to describe what had happened to her. 'At night, were you victims of sexual abuse?', asked Mbacké Fall, the chief prosecutor. 'I can't reply to that. My children are watching me on the television', she replied. 'But sexual abuse happened there?' Houawa remained silent, and then answered: 'Death was preferable to what we had to live through.'[22]

But it was the testimony of Khadidja Hassan Zidane, a beautiful woman in her early fifties wearing a striking red and black headscarf, which was to create perhaps the greatest shockwaves of the entire case. Khadidja claimed to have been arrested and taken to the presidency, where her brother, a pilot, was already being held on suspicion of links to Libya. Seemingly unintimidated and turning down the offer to give her testimony in a closed session, Khadidja explained that she had been the victim of sexual violence at the presidency and offered to take her clothes off to show the court where she had been stabbed in the leg and genitals by her attacker. It took several gentle but firm questions from Judge Kam to establish exactly what had happened to her, but eventually a clearly uncomfortable Khadidja revealed that Hissène Habré himself had raped her four times. The former president was sitting just metres away from her still hidden among his gleaming white robes, with his right hand inclined against his face, index finger extended, staring unflinchingly ahead as she recounted her story. She told the court that Habré had been wearing fatigues on the night of the attack, and had asked her to sit down before pulling her by her hair and attacking her. She said the first two times she had resisted but then after that she had lost the will to fight him. Her account caused a number of uncomfortable reactions in the courtroom, as did the one hour, forty minute long cross-examination by the court-appointed defence team on the second day. Khadidja responded to the defence team with determination, her voice rising and becoming irritated as Mounir Ballal forcefully challenged the fact that she could not remember specific dates, including her date of birth and age. They queried a number of apparent contradictions between her 'procès verbal' (sworn statement) and her court testimony, and asked why she had not revealed this dark secret before. She told the court that it wasn't important to her what date it was or how old she was, and the shame of the rapes was such that she had never told any of the investigators before this moment what had happened. At one point she was subject to a cross-examination by a lawyer for the civil parties who posed the bizarre question, 'Why have you brought a photograph with you? Is it to show that your beauty was at the source of all your problems?', to which she replied, 'I brought my photo so that Habré would recognise me, because old age has not been kind to me'. She told the defence lawyers that the DDS was like the three monkeys, one who sees no evil, one who hears no evil and one who speaks no evil.

The evidence of sexual violence did not stop there. On several other occasions women testified to the extreme cruel and degrading treatment they had experienced. Fatimé Limane, who was pregnant in detention, described how soldiers had inserted bayonets into her vagina, killing her unborn child. Garba Akhaya testified about a female cellmate receiving electric shocks to her breasts and genitals which left her unable to walk. Stories emerged of several women being routinely raped and abused by soldiers and prison guards. Others had been forced to give birth in prison without any medical assistance. Fatimé Sakine testified about her treatment in 'Les Locaux', where she had been held with around fifteen other women. She was taken out of her cell to the office of the director of the DDS Saleh Younouss to be abused so often that she earned the sobriquet 'Mme Saleh Younouss'. Clement Abaifouta claimed that there was even a special room set aside in the prison where the women would be raped.

There was similar treatment for the men. When Souleymane Guengueng finally took to the stand to describe his torture, the court was gripped by his testimony. After a twenty-five-year battle and such humiliating treatment in prison, this was clearly an emotional moment for him, yet he is a remarkably gentle man. He walked slowly to the stand, took his time with his story and paused reflectively, as if remembering some of those who had died alongside him. He told the court in a composed and clear voice about his experience in the Camp des Martyrs and the Camp de Gendarmerie prison where he was subject to being hung by the testicles and beaten with electrical cables.

His co-detainee Robert Gambier's voice tailed off into sobs and he wiped away his tears with a handkerchief as he told the court how he had been repeatedly attacked in his genital area. Ahmat Maki Outman described how he had seen DDS agents inserting pieces of wood into his cellmate's penises. French doctor Hélène Jaffe, now eighty-three years old, gave serious testimony at the bar about her work, which began in Chad in the 1990s, giving physical and psychological support to victims of torture. She talked of the signs of torture and mistreatment she had uncovered, including scars and untreated wounds, which had caused many of the victims constant generalised pain. She testified she had treated many men who showed signs of sexual abuse, and had cured a number of them who had suffered sexual dysfunction as a result.

The testimony of Khadidja Hassan Zidane was all the more shocking because she had never made these allegations of Habré himself raping her in any of the preparatory witness sessions before the EAC officially opened. Talk of sexual abuse and rape during Habré's rule was common, but there had not been a specific focus on the women's stories as the case was being prepared. Their evidence appeared to have been gathered in a similar manner to all the other witness statements, without being given specialist attention, and the women who had made allegations of sexual abuse – an extremely shameful admission in a society like Chad – had not been offered any official support. Seemingly unwilling to reveal their dark secrets until absolutely forced to, it was as if the experience of being called to Dakar to testify, the immensity and gravity of an official court process, had triggered something in the women's minds which had convinced them that now was finally the time to break the silence they had kept so painfully for almost thirty years.

These unexpected revelations appeared to cause a degree of soul-searching on the part of the court's legal team. The founding statute of the EAC had given the court jurisdiction to try cases involving crimes against humanity, which included 'Rape, sexual slavery, enforced prostitution, enforced sterilisation or any other form of sexual violence of comparable gravity'.[23] However, the indictment issued against Habré by the investigating judges in February 2015 – on charges of war crimes, crimes against humanity and torture – did not explicitly charge Habré with rape or other forms of sexual violence as a war crime, crime against humanity or act of genocide or torture. This was an omission seized upon by a number of human rights and campaign groups. In October 2015, as the trial was underway, a coalition of seventeen groups, including the Panzi Foundation of Dr Denis Mukwege, who has received numerous prizes for his work supporting victims of sexual violence, wrote an open letter to the EAC to express their dismay that the court was failing to pay proper attention to the 'systemic' use of sexual violence – including against men – throughout the 1980s in Chad. 'Not to prosecute Hissène Habré for sexual crimes would be a missed historical opportunity; it would deprive a large number of victims of the recognition of the crimes they suffered because they are women', the groups argued.[24]

The dramatic impact of the women's testimony, particularly the allegations that even children had been raped and abused, encouraged other lawyers and legal support groups around the world to make a last-minute attempt to persuade the EAC to shift its focus. Just days before the last witness took the stand in December 2015, a group of sixteen lawyers, including the South African Justice Richard Goldstone, who had served at the ICTY, Patricia Sellers, an advisor to the ICC, and Madeleine Rees, the secretary general of the Women's International League for Peace and Freedom, sent an 'amicus curiae brief' to the court asking for the charges against the former president to be revised in light of new details arising from the testimony of sexual violence survivors. The brief set out the options at the judge's disposal, based on both the provisions of the tribunal's own statute and customary international law.[25] The brief was prepared by the Human Rights Centre at the University of California, Berkeley, led by lawyer Kim Thuy Seelinger. It asked the court to examine the allegations of rape and sexual slavery and to 'properly characterise them as crimes against humanity, war crimes and acts of torture' using customary international law.[26] It gave ample examples of applicable case law, including how rape and crimes of sexual violence had been incorporated into the prosecutions at Nuremberg and also under the ICTR and ICTY. Although the brief was initially welcomed on receipt by the presiding judge Kam, there was some concern among the campaigners that its purpose had been misunderstood. It was finally agreed it could be used to advise the lawyers for the civil parties, and was indeed used in the civil parties' summing up submission. However, it never made it on to the record, apparently because of a limit on the number of pages allowed. 'We are glad at least that it seems our submission will influence the court's work indirectly', said a disappointed Kim Thuy Seelinger at the time.[27] The campaigners and lawyers were to have to wait until the verdict in May 2016 to see if their hard work was to influence in any way the EAC's conclusions on rape and sexual abuse.

The last three witnesses were called to testify before the EAC between 14 and 16 December 2015. The court heard from Oumar Goudja, a Zaghawa businessman who had been arrested in 1989 when returning from Cameroon on suspicion of supporting Déby and Djamous. Subjected to whippings, electrical shocks and beatings, he was imprisoned for the rest of Habré's rule in 'Les Locaux' and claimed to have spent time in Cellule C with the brother of Goukouni Oueddei, Chad's former president whom Habré had ousted in 1982. The final witness explained how a number of BSIR missions had taken place under the order of the president. He claimed that Habré was 'up to date with everything that happened every morning and lunchtime'.[28]

His testimony brought to an end an extraordinary three months of gruelling evidence which had left many people's minds reeling. Eighty witnesses and victims had testified, along with ten expert witnesses. Exhausted, the lawyers, judges, civil parties and victims listened as Judge Kam closed the court until the summation of evidence due in February 2016. The evidence had surely shown beyond any doubt the senselessness and viciousness of the violence and human rights abuses which had occurred in Chad throughout the 1980s, as well as given a hint as to the national scale of what had taken place. It seemed inconceivable that the EAC could conclude anything other than guilty. However the big question at the back of everyone's minds was, had the personal responsibility of Hissène Habré himself been convincingly proved? 'There was no smoking gun', said Reed Brody at the time.[29]

Many attempts had been made during the witness phase of the trial to provide evidence of a direct link between the president and human rights violations beyond the general provisions of the command responsibility clause. Hand-writing expert Tobin Tanaka was brought in to give his opinion on whether a number of written orders taken from the pile of DDS documents could be traced back to the president. The most notorious of these was a chilling letter in response to an ICRC request to visit prisoners of war which read 'Aucun prisonnier de guerre ne doit quitter la maison d'arrêt sauf cas de décès' (No prisoner of war will leave the prison apart from those who have died). Tanaka confirmed in his expert opinion that the handwriting on this letter matched that on a number of documents known to have been signed by the president. There was of course the infamous presidential decree no. 5 of January 1983 which created the DDS, and ten witnesses testified to either having met Habré in prison, or having been sent there personally by him.

HRW's Olivier Bercault, who together with Reed Brody had discovered the enormous cache of DDS documents discarded in the former DDS headquarters in N'Djamena, had confirmed in court that they had uncovered 1265 direct communications between the DDS and the president concerning the individual situations of 898 detainees. He singled out one document which had detailed the supply of fraudulent toilet tissue and a few pots of tomatoes which had been seized by the DDS, as evidence of the level of detail Habré had been given.[30] The court also heard detailed evidence of the counter-attack against Faya Largeau, which had been taken by the GUNT in 1983 – numerous witnesses testified that it was Habré himself who had commanded the FANT in battle and that he had been present for significant periods of time. Mianmbaye Djetoldia Dakoye testified that he had seen the former president in the room where a number of POWs were kept and had heard him telling guards that the captives were 'toddlers' and that the soldiers could 'do what you want' with them.[31] Also crucial was the case of the massacre at the village of Ngalo in the south, where seventy people had been killed by the FANT in 1985. According to one witness, the troops had returned a week later with a direct message from Habré claiming that he had not ordered the massacre – which was used by the defence team to demonstrate that Habré had tried to stop abuses. However, according to the witnesses, the president had ordered that the two soldiers who had allowed the massacre to happen should themselves be executed as proof of his goodwill to the villagers. Which they were.

Summing up

On 8 February 2016 the lawyers at the EAC began a week-long summing up. Two months had passed since the end of the dramatic witness testimony phase, but emotions were still high. During the summing up phase the lawyers for the civil parties again returned to the question of demonstrating beyond all doubt that they had proved the link between the former president and the crimes. Confidently marching up to the stand, Jacqueline Moudeina presented the court with an 'organigramme', an organisational chart to explain how the

DDS had been set up. It showed Habré at the centre of the secret police with a direct link of communication to key figures such as Saleh Younouss and El Djonto. Chadian lawyer Maitre Phillipe Houssine, also for the civil parties, reminded the court how Saleh Younouss, a former director of the DDS, had told the 1992 Commissions of Enquiry how Habré had personally shaped the goals of the DDS, that 'Little by little, the president himself gave a new orientation to the directorate and made it into an instrument of terror'.[32] El Djonto had told the same enquiry that it was the president himself who had given the orders. The court was reminded of the numerous testimonies which had attested to seeing Habré himself at the headquarters of the DDS close to the presidential palace, how he had the power to name the directors (including for example his own nephew Guihini Korei) and viewed the DDS as his own. Swiss lawyer Alain Werner, director of the advocacy group Civitas Maxima and who represented the civil parties, brandished the note found in the DDS archive describing the agency as the 'cobweb which will cover the entire Chadian territory' and the 'eyes and ears of the President'. He also drew attention to an interview the former president gave to the Chadian newspaper Al-Watan in the 1980s, declaring that his enemies would be unmasked, destroyed and 'crushed'. At times the summing up by the assembled lawyers acting on behalf of the civil parties verged on melodramatic. Chadian lawyer Maitre Laminal Ndintamadji reminded the court of the incontestable facts of soldiers gunned down at Ambing, but went on to claim that the DDS was like the Gestapo and compared Habré to Hitler. Civil parties' lawyer Assane Dioma Ndiaye said that what happened in Chad was worse than Rwanda and Congo. Again, the issue of the lack of specific focus on rape and sexual violence in the trial was brought to the attention of the judges.

The civil parties' summing up was followed by the conclusions of the prosecution team. Chief Prosecutor Mbacké Fall concluded that the evidence was overwhelming and reminded the court that the DDS had been created by a presidential decree. The prosecution argued that Habré was individually responsible through his complicity and incitement of these activities, even if he did not personally carry all of them out. Fall called for a sentence of life imprisonment for the former president, and the confiscation of his possessions and money. Prosecutor Moustapha Ka again clarified the legal concept of command responsibility ('supérieure hiérarchique'), which meant that as head of state and the army, Habré was the ultimate guarantor of Chad's international treaty obligations including the UN CAT. It was argued that he had not done enough to stop crimes committed on his watch, and that on that alone the proof of his guilt was 'undeniable'.[33]

On the final day, the court-appointed defence team spoke. Their defence argument was in part based on challenging the credibility of a number of key witnesses, for example criticising the work of the head of the 1992 Truth Commission Mahamat Hassan Abakar. Their second strategy was to contend that it was impossible to prove that the former president had been aware of everything that was happening at any moment across Chad's immense territory, including the massacres in the south which they claimed had occurred during his Hajj pilgrimage in 1984. At the end of their evidence Judge Gustave Gberdao Kam closed the session and informed the court that he was retiring to deliberate the verdict, which would be delivered on 30 May 2016.

Verdict and sentencing

On the day of the verdict, a Monday, the atmosphere in the main courtroom in Dakar's Palais de Justice was tense. Had the prosecution and civil parties done enough to prove Habré's direct responsibility for the crimes committed by the DDS in Chad in the 1980s? So far the EAC had proved remarkably disciplined, maintaining a tight schedule, but there were worries that the verdict could be delayed. How would the various parties react? Would Hissène Habré finally break his silence? 'We couldn't contemplate the possibility that he would not be found guilty – the evidence was so strong', said Reed Brody.[34]

Normally we prepare two press releases in case the case goes the wrong way – like in Citizen Kane when he has two front pages ready to go, one announcing his political win and the other his failure to win – but this time we didn't have a press release saying we had lost. We were confident, but nevertheless the judges had never showed their hand, there had been mistakes in the evidence and things which had not been brought out. We were worried he might only get five years or released with a caution.

In the end these fears were mostly assuaged. Judge Kam's address was short and to the point. Habré was found guilty on the basis of his participation in a joint criminal enterprise of crimes against humanity, consisting of the underlying crimes of murder, summary executions, forced disappearances, torture and cruel and inhuman acts. He was convicted of the autonomous crime of torture. The Chamber further concluded that Habré was liable under command responsibility of war crimes, consisting of murder, cruel and inhumane treatment, illegal detention and torture. He was acquitted of the charge of the illegal transfer of prisoners. He was further found guilty, through individual criminal responsibility, of ordering the executions of soldiers at Ngalo in his position of commander in chief of the army.

There was big news on the requalification of charges relating to rape and sexual violence which had been omitted from the original charges. Firstly the former president was found guilty of directly committing rape and torture against Khadidja Hassan Zidane, the woman who had so shockingly accused him of personally abusing her on four occasions. Despite the defence's assertion that her testimony had been unreliable, the court concluded that the reason she had remained silent on the rapes prior to the case reaching court had been because of her modesty and that she was scared of the impact on her family. They reminded the court that she had told a friend about the attacks in the immediate aftermath. In terms of the type of responsibility Habré bore for the other crimes of sexual violence in evidence the court noted that while rape, sexual violence and slavery probably fell outside the common criminal purpose of the joint criminal enterprise, which was to repress any and all opposition to his rule, they nonetheless constituted a foreseeable risk willingly undertaken by Habré. He was therefore found guilty of these crimes under the so-called 'third category' of joint criminal enterprise, where liability is based on the foreseeability and the voluntary taking of a risk that a crime outside the common enterprise will be carried out.[35] However, the EAC failed to convict him of the use of rape as a war crime.

The judge spoke of thousands of victims and the central role that the former president had played in controlling the decisions of the DDS. He specifically remarked upon Habré's dismissive attitude toward the court through his persistent wearing of a turban covering his face, and his refusal to speak or to stand when the court opened or closed sessions. As Hissène Habré was given a sentence of life imprisonment, with fifteen days for his defence team to prepare an appeal, he simply breathed heavily and raised his eyes to the ceiling.

The gathered victims, witnesses and legal representatives for the civil parties could barely contain their delight. A few seconds after Judge Kam finished speaking, the courtroom slowly began to break into cries of joy, ululations and singing. Clement Abaifouta, Jacqueline Moudeina, Delphine Djiraibe and Souleymane Guengueng smiled wearily, hundreds of camera-phones flashed and people pushed through to shake hands and embrace each other. Habré was led from the court by his Senegalese friends, his clenched fist yet again raised in defiance.[36] It was hard to believe that this was really the end of a twenty-five-year battle. 'It was so worth it', said Jacqueline Moudeina. 'I felt so proud that day. I never let it go. I knew one day we would get there.'[37]

It was several weeks before the full written judgment was released, a 681-page document which recounted all the evidence that had been submitted to the court. This document gave the full legal and historical background to the trial and detailed the case and international law and legal classification on which the founding statute had been based. It returned in detail to the thorny question of individual responsibility in the light of the fact that the original indictment had been for Habré and his five co-accused on the basis of 'joint criminal enterprise', given that the five DDS co-accused had not been present in Dakar for the trial. Eventually it concluded that Habré had been a part of a joint criminal enterprise, including the BSIR and the DDS which was designed to crack down on opponents, and again found Habré responsible for its creation through the issuing of the 18 October 1982 presidential decree and his naming of all the top agents at the DDS. The defence argument that the body had been under the control of the Minister of the Interior was dismissed. It concluded that Habré had 'exercised direct and full control over the DDS from its creation' and it had been proved that he received daily detailed dossiers of what was happening in the prisons.[38]

On the question of command responsibility, the judgment returned to the requirements that the accused should be found responsible if he knew or had reason to know that a crime had been committed by subordinates under his watch and that he had not taken sufficient measures to prevent that crime taking place. The court found that on the basis of his role as head of the armed forces and from 1986 as Minister of Defence, it had been sufficiently proved that there was a direct line of command between him and the DDS. It concluded that he had direct responsibility over the DDS and the FANT and this had allowed him to have the required level of knowledge about what the agencies were doing. It found that he had been personally present during several battles against the GUNT near Faya Largeau in 1983 and had at times personally directed the FANT, and that there was no doubt he had been aware of the number of prisoners of war taken and of their poor treatment by his soldiers. In addition it concluded that he had reason to know that the massacres of prisoners of war such as the atrocity at Ambing might take place. In effect the court had proven that Habré had been responsible for the human rights abuses in Chad in the 1980s under three modes of responsibility – command responsibility, personal liability and as part of a joint criminal enterprise. However it is important to bear in mind that if the court was sufficiently able to prove command responsibility – which it appears to have been able to do, and indeed the defence did not even try to contest this responsibility[39] – this alone would have been sufficient proof of Habré's guilt.

Calls for compensation

Once the dust settled on the verdict, the EAC turned its attention to the difficult question of compensation for the victims. All the lawyers for the various civil party groupings had made claims to the court for 'adequate, effective and rapid' reparations for 1049 direct and 3684 indirect victims, commensurate with the level of seriousness of the crimes committed against them.[40] HRW had previously argued that similar compensation schemes had been effective for victims of human rights abuses in Argentina and Chile in the 1970s, and that South Africa's Truth and Reconciliation Committee had offered similar suggestions. Habré's victims were classified into groups according to what had happened to them – for example, victims of rape, victims of sexual enslavement and victims of arbitrary arrests. Lawyers representing Clement Abaifouta and colleagues also submitted a claim for 30% of the total value of money available for reparations to be put towards a collective fund which would erect a monument and museum to the victims of Habré in Chad and ensure that Habré's rule should be taught as a historical period in the nation's schools. In fact the issue of 'restitution, compensation and rehabilitation' collectively or individually had been mandated in the EAC Statute and is a principle of international law.[41] The statute also ordered that a Trust Fund should be

restorative justice

established to invite voluntary contributions from foreign donors and NGOs to support the victims.

It was another two months before Judge Kam recalled the court to announce the conclusions of the EAC on victim compensation. The court ordered Habré to pay a total of around €81 million ($97 million) to his victims, with amounts ranging from €30,490 ($36,600) for rape victims, to €22,865 ($27,440) for victims of torture, arbitrary detention and each mistreated former prisoner of war and escapee, and €15,243 ($18,290) for each indirect victim, which included mostly the relatives of people who had disappeared or who were imprisoned and tortured. These sums were given a lukewarm welcome by several lawyers for the civil parties, such as Jacqueline Moudeina, who had initially called for around €270 million ($324 million) in compensation. She was also disappointed that no award had been made on the basis of collective compensation, and that some victims had been unable to register as civil parties or to sufficiently prove their identity and consequently had been denied compensation. Others were more philosophical: 'Money will never bring back my friends', Souleymane Guengueng told the website Justice Hub, 'but money is important to heal the wounds, to take victims out of poverty and to show that we have rights that must be recognised.'[42]

Despite the quick verdict by the court, the issue of where the compensation money was to come from would become much more lingering. Little progress has been made in enforcing an order made by the N'Djamena court in 2015 at the conclusion of the trial of the DDS agents that the Chadian state was liable for 75 billion CFCA ($125 million) in damages, particularly as Chad continues to undergo a severe economic crisis sparked by the low global oil price. At the time of writing, there has also been little progress in establishing the victims' Trust Fund to invite voluntary donations by foreign partners. One of the major stumbling blocks is that the EAC Statute is vague about exactly whose responsibility it is to ensure the Trust Fund is established, and there continue to be questions about where it should be hosted.[43] Although the body was created on paper by the AU in July 2016, once the EAC Appeals Chamber was dissolved it was ruled that the issue should fall to a 'comité de pilotage' (steering committee). However, this body has yet to be set up, with several meetings at the AU scheduled and a donors' conference postponed. The UK-based human rights organisation Redress, which helps torture victims obtain justice and reparation, sent an 'amicus curiae' brief to the EAC with advice on how previous such Trust Funds, including one set up in South Africa after the TRC, have been established. According to Nader Diab from Redress, the EAC's temporary status has made chasing reparations challenging:

> The problem we have is that the court is in one country and is making an order for reparations in another country (Chad). This raises issues of sovereignty.[44]

It has also proved exceedingly difficult to trace Habré's assets. The issue of recovering money stolen by Habré fell by the wayside as the EAC was forced to limit the scope of its investigations through lack of budget and a tight timescale. The paper trail uncovered by Mahamat Hassan Abakar during the early 1990s, which mainly focused on the night Habré ordered his brother to cash a cheque at the BEAC before his flight into exile, had only identified about €6 million ($7.2 million) as having been stolen. The Truth Commission had also identified a few other small sums including a $1 million gift from Saddam Hussein to the former president. Although these were significant sums in Chad in 1990 when its GDP was barely about $0.5 billion, they constitute nowhere near the amount ordered by the EAC for the reparations. When the compensation verdict was announced, only one upmarket house belonging to Habré and two small bank accounts had been seized by the court, totalling less than €900,000 ($1.08 million).[45] Beyond that, remarkably little information exists about what happened to the money. A team of HRW researchers has so far uncovered little of significance. Twenty-five years of political obscurity in Dakar had been a long time for Hissène Habré to make himself comfortable through a complex network of investments, often in his family members' names, and over the years there had been numerous accusations (see Chapter 2) that he had been able to use his ill-gotten gains to pay off a range of legal and political figures to ensure that he would never be brought to trial. Nader Diab says that tracing assets is usually done by specialist legal teams, but these are often extremely expensive endeavours. Although there may be a possibility to engage a UN body such as the UN Office on Drugs and Crime to conduct an investigation, so far little has been done. There is also a tricky (and unresolved) moral question of whether assets stolen from the state (as Habré's millions were) should be returned to the state, or granted to the victims. Without a permanent body to monitor and follow up on these outstanding issues it seems hard to imagine the victims being granted compensation any time soon. 'I'm amazed by how little we know about Habré's money', said Nader Diab.[46] 'We can usually start these things with a few leads, but in this case we really don't have much.'

The appeal

In December 2016, the three Senegalese court-appointed defence lawyers formally notified the EAC that they wished to lodge an appeal against Hissène Habré's conviction and life sentence. A formal hearing for the appeal was scheduled to start on 9 January 2017. Once again, Moudeina, Abaifouta, Guengueng and Brody, plus a handful of stalwart victims, packed their bags and headed for Dakar. The Appeals Chamber consisted of a presiding judge, the Malian Wafi Ouagadeye, and two 'assessor' judges, Matar Ndiaye and Bara Gueye, both Senegalese, who were all appointed by the AU. It was from the start an odd process in that Habré himself appeared not to want to appeal. Continuing his policy of staunch non-cooperation from his prison cell, he simply refused to talk, but the lawyers decided to push ahead anyway and launch the appeal on his behalf.

The EAC Statute allowed appeals based on procedural grounds, factual errors and when the rights of the accused could be said to have been violated, and indeed the defence submission centred around mostly objections on technical grounds. The most significant of these was the claim that one of the Senegalese judges on the EAC bench, Amady Diouf, did not have the requisite ten years of experience demanded by the EAC founding statute. There were also objections to the fact that the Belgian investigating judge Daniel Fransen had been allowed to testify in front of the court, violating Senegal's separation between investigating and prosecuting judges and highlighting a perceived confusion over whether Senegalese or international law should take precedence. There was also an objection to the fact that victims had been allowed to attend the court before giving testimony, which the defence argued could 'contaminate' their evidence,[47] and an objection to the fact that the evidence of Khadidja Zidane, the woman who had directly accused the former president of raping her, had been allowed even though she had not formally made the allegations in her pre-trial sworn statement.[48]

More generally some of the themes of the defence line during the Trial Chamber emerged in their appeal submission. These included the idea of a conspiracy between the 1992 Truth Commission, the Court and HRW, the question marks over who was ultimately responsible for the repression carried out by the army during the Black September period of 1984, and the argument that the DDS had in fact been put under the control of the then Minister of Interior by the president. There was also a general claim that the rights of Habré had been violated through various procedural errors, including mistakes in identifying victims. At the same time the civil parties had also lodged an appeal before the Appeals Chamber claiming that the reparations awarded by the court in

July 2016 had been insufficient and should be reviewed. They called again for an award of collective reparations.

The Appeals hearing lasted four days, and rather than being seen as an easily dismissed action in fact rather concerned the victims' groups. Jacqueline Moudeina told me on her return to Chad following the hearing in mid-January 2017 she was worried that 'he may get a reduction in sentence to something insignificant like five years', and Reed Brody expressed concern that any lighter sentence could undo much of the healing inspired by the original conviction. These fears seem to have been compounded by the declaration of Senegal's Minister of Justice Sidiki Kaba, the day after the guilty verdict in May 2016, that Habré could be in line for a presidential pardon from Macky Sall once the EAC court had been wound up.[49] Furthermore, the EAC founding statute stated that if convicted, Habré should serve out his sentence in Senegal *or another country which is a member of the AU*, a point which led to further speculation that he could be transferred to a third country such as Morocco to serve out his penalty, possibly benefiting from more lenient conditions such as a house arrest where his family could join him.

In the end, as with the original conviction, these fears were unfounded. On Thursday 27 April 2017 the long saga of the battle to bring Hissène Habré to justice finally came to an end. In a short hearing which Habré had characteristically refused to attend, the Appeals Chamber of the EAC upheld the majority of the guilty verdicts issued against him, rejecting all of the defence team's appeal based on technical and procedural error. The only fly in the ointment was the decision to overturn the conviction for the direct commission of rape against Khadidja Zidane, the case which had electrified the court when she had unexpectedly accused him of personally attacking her four times in her testimony during the EAC witness phase. In explaining his decision, Malian Judge Wafi Ouagadeye said that although the court believed Zidane's account, the conviction could not be upheld as the EAC Statute did not permit adding new facts that were not in the original indictment.[50] In confirming the majority of the verdict, the court concluded that there was to be no reduction in sentence even given the rejection of the rape conviction. Habré finally seemed condemned to spend the rest of his life behind bars.

For the victims there was a great sense of relief. Standing outside the court wearing his trademark chunky gold ring and dark trilby hat, leaning on the cane which after the years in jail he now needs to walk, Souleymane Guengueng told reporters, 'I have been fighting for this day since I walked out of prison more than 26 years ago. Today, I finally feel free'.[51] However, the overturning of the rape conviction left a bitter taste for some, especially after what had been hailed as the court's notable success in requalifying the original charges – which had omitted rape and sexual violence – to include rape as a crime against humanity. The Khadidja case had been uncharted ground as soon as she had unexpectedly made her allegations in court. The Appeals Chamber judgment pointedly stressed that it found her a credible witness, but the fact that the conviction was overturned has led to some suspicion that there may have been political pressure applied to spare Habré the shame of going down in history as a convicted rapist. 'I'm still pleased that the sexual violence aspects of this case were acknowledged by the court – it's a major piece of jurisprudence', Kim Thuy Seelinger, the Director of the Sexual Violence Program at the Human Rights Center, University of California Berkeley School of Law, told me following the verdict. 'But I still don't understand why sexual violence as a war crime was rejected by the court. There remain a number of unclear points.'[52]

The Appeals verdict also made a number of rulings on the reparations issue, which may now provide impetus to make serious progress in compensating the victims according to the court mandate in July 2016. In responding to the appeal lodged by the civil parties, the verdict opened the possibility for victims who had not participated in the proceedings or who had been unable to prove their identity to now apply for reparations from the Trust Fund, broadening the rules for those who qualified for compensation to include those who had been unable to constitute a 'civil party'. In accordance with the expected rise in the number of claimants, the judgment revised the amount of compensation awarded upwards from around €81 million to around €125 million ($97–150 million). The Appeals Chamber called on the AU to activate the Trust Fund, and instructed the Trust Fund to implement the reparations order and begin the search for Habré's elusive assets. There remains a lack of clarity over who has ultimate responsibility for this Trust Fund, although legal queries will be dealt with by the Tribunal de Grande Instance in Dakar. At the time of writing there has yet to be a concrete decision regarding its launch.[53] The Appeals Chamber again declined to award collective reparations, including funds for a memorial to the victims and a museum – a key demand of the civil parties appeal brief. It also declined to address the sovereignty issues regarding the award of reparations by a court based in Senegal to victims based in Chad, or the enforcement of the compensation awarded to the victims by the N'Djamena court in 2015. In early 2017, Redress and its partners sent a letter to the UN Special Rapporteur on Truth, Justice, Reparation and Guarantees of Non-recurrence together with a submission by Jacqueline Moudeina, urging the Special Rapporteur to intervene with the Chadian government concerning the government's failure to implement these reparations. In November 2017 Redress also supported Clement Abaifouta on behalf of 7000 victims in filing a human rights complaint against the government of Chad before the African Commission on Human and Peoples' Rights.

'Without coercive powers or an agreement with Chad the implementation of the reparations cannot take place', said Nader Diab from Redress shortly after the verdict. 'There is no hard law to bind Chad to consent to anything.'[54] Although the Appeals verdict has laid the foundations for the Trust Fund to be established and has provided lawyers fighting for the money with more effective tools, the issue of implementing compensation awards looks set to remain for some time to come.

Chapter 4

HEALING AT HOME

The victims' reaction

It may well be the most filmed courtyard in N'Djamena. Tucked away under the concrete legs of a new flyover built by the Chinese – big investors in Chad's southern oilfields – the headquarters of the 'Association des victimes des crimes du régime Habré' is a small adobe building with a heavy gate that seems almost constantly in use. Each time I have visited there has been a quiet hum of activity coming from the courtyard which has featured in numerous documentaries and news reports over the years. On this particular bright and sunny January morning, a group of women was seated on colourful raffia mats on the dusty floor, slowly pouring tea and sharing bread, sewing and chatting, batting away the flies in the unseasonal heat. A few men were sitting on white plastic chairs murmuring. A simple tin roof was all that protected the assembled crowd from the burning sun.

Arrangements are sometimes informal in Chad and I'd assumed the rendez-vous at 10am would not be taken literally, but it was immediately obvious when I arrived that everyone had been waiting some time for me. Yet people only smiled and welcomed me generously. I recognised several of the women from Mahamat-Saleh Haroun's film *Hissène Habré: A Chadian Tragedy*.

I returned to Chad in January 2017 to find out how the indefatigable victims of Habré were feeling eight months after the verdict. I wanted to know if they've been able to move on with their lives.

Had the horrors of the past begun to fade from memory? Had Habré – a figure of terror for many – been diminished and neutralised in their imaginations? The day I arrived was the day following the closing of the appeals hearing in Dakar and everyone had been watching nervously, fearing that the former president could get a reduction in his sentence. Jean Noyoma Kovousouma, vice president of the association and Clement Abaifouta's deputy, shook my hand and gave me a warm smile. I recognised him from the videos of the court proceedings in Dakar and recalled his testimony about his seven months at the Camp des Martyrs prison after being accused of being a Libyan collaborator. He pulled up a plastic chair behind a desk in a concrete room inside the building which became my makeshift office for the next two days. Hawa Guankargue, herself a victim, brought me a large bottle of water, a metal dish containing some soggy salad and a bottle of sweet pineapple yoghurt drink. There was a poster advertising Mahamat-Saleh Haroun's film on the wall. I got down to work.

The overwhelming impression I had from speaking to the twenty or so victims who gathered over two days to tell me their experiences was one of enduring patience. I was conscious that they had told their stories time and time again to every journalist and film-maker who has tramped through N'Djamena over the years, and yet still they came. Many of these victims and relatives of the disappeared had travelled at their own expense to be present for at least some of the witness phase of the trial in Dakar. It seems to have been the most extraordinary thing for them to have seen Hissène Habré in the dock, and to have had their stories taken seriously and their suffering acknowledged. 'It was horrible to see him there', said Khaltouma Daba, whose husband was arrested by the DDS and disappeared forever, 'but we were satisfied that we got justice in the end. It has been a great healing for me'.

'I cried when I saw him there. It was the first time I've cried in public', said Naomi Minguebeye, a beautiful woman in her fifties who was widowed and found her husband's body bound and riddled with bullets four days after he was arrested by the DDS in 1984 during Black September. 'Everyone in Chad needed to see the trial. I think it will change things here, and in the rest of Africa. Now even presidents know they can't get away with murder.'

'The trial liberated me. It was like I had a hunger that could never be sated. I had to see it happen to be free', said Fatimeh Tchanjdoum.

> I never believed he would actually be there; he used to be like a God in Chad and everyone was terrorised by him. I saw him sitting there twitching and fiddling with his scarf, he was obviously troubled. It's given me hope and changed my life. Since the trial I started to gain weight again after many years, and I feel calm in my mind.

'Everyone used to laugh at us victims', said Mahamat Moussa Mahamat, a teacher, wearing a typically Chadian white boubou and turban. 'They thought we were crazy to think he would ever be judged. Now we're not scared anymore. This has changed everything – now we can have confidence in our friends and families again.'

But despite the fact that Habré's conviction and life sentence were deeply satisfying with regard to correcting the historical injustice, many of those I spoke to in N'Djamena continue to be frustrated by the lack of progress on the promise of compensation. As explored in Chapter 3, part of the EAC judgment delivered in May 2016 promised nearly 5000 direct victims and relatives amounts ranging from €15,000 to €30,000 ($18,000–36,000). In addition, the Chadian government was ordered by a court in N'Djamena to pay half of the $150 million compensation promised to victims after the conclusion of the trial of the former DDS agents in early 2015. Although these were both positive moves, there has so far been little progress in securing the money promised. The EAC has struggled to trace Habré's assets, and a Trust Fund for his victims mandated by the court's statute has yet to be established. The Chadian government has also been unable to honour its commitments; it has been in the grip of a severe financial crisis since late 2014 when the world oil price collapsed leaving state finances in tatters. The country is dependent on oil money for 70% of government revenues and the government has been forced to slash budgets, cancel infrastructure projects and suspend salary payments for civil servants, teachers and magistrates. Paying compensation to Habré's victims is not high on the priority list, and it looks unlikely anyone will receive the money any time soon.

Many of the victims expressed a feeling that these delays mean that justice is not yet complete, and that some kind of restitution is necessary. 'I need that money. I lost everything when my husband disappeared and I've only been able to bring up my six kids with the help from family members', said Fatimah Oumar, whose Nigerian husband disappeared in 1989 after being accused of supporting Idriss Déby and the Zaghawa rebellion. 'The government doesn't talk to us. They don't want to help us with money. Every day I go and sit near the bridge at Kousseri to sell peanut oil. It's all I've got.'

'I used to be worth thousands of dollars. I used to be a big businessman', said Hassan Ibrahim Adam, a slight elderly man who walks with a cane. He was taken prisoner after fighting with the GUNT near Adé and Goz Beida in 1984. 'They took everything from my house after I was imprisoned. All my goods. Look at me now, I'm nothing, I'm diminished. I can't forgive him after everything I've been through.'

'If I have an accident in my car you pay me insurance. Is a human life not worth that much?', said Mokhtar Abdellah, whose elder brother disappeared in Faya Largeau in 1987. 'Habré stole our money and we want it back. The EAC needs to work harder to recover the money. Why is there nothing in the Trust Fund? I don't accept that there is no money available for us.'[1]

Wider society

Beyond the networks of direct victims, witnesses and bereaved families who have been adept at getting their voices heard around the world, it is harder to assess what the impact of the Habré trial has been on wider Chadian society. Although the EAC Outreach Consortium (see below) has made available several reports about the reactions and emotions they encountered while carrying out their work, so far no serious academic research into the implications of the trial in Chad itself has been carried out. Much of what we hear about Chadian views on the verdict comes from the small group of now fairly famous activists, lawyers and victims, figures such as Jacqueline Moudeina, Clement Abaifouta and Souleymane Guengueng. (I chose to visit Guengueng and Abaifouta's group as they are the best known and most accessible, although there is in fact another prominent victims' group which has not achieved the same level of media attention as Guengueng and Abaifouta's group, leading to some questions about who chooses to speak for victims and how a dominant narrative emerges.)

In order to reach more deeply into the impact of the trial on those not *directly* affected, I decided to ask a research assistant in Chad, Augustin Zusanne, to collect a small sample of opinions from ordinary Chadians from all walks of life. I asked him to pose five questions about the trial to twenty Chadians in N'Djamena, rich and poor, young and old, women and men, employed and unemployed. These questions were: 'Did you follow the Habré trial and why?'; 'What impact has the Habré trial had on Chadian justice?'; 'Should the other five co-accused have been sent to Dakar and why?'; 'Could anything have been done differently?' and 'What do you think about the role of the US and France in keeping Habré in power?' Of course this survey was extremely limited in scope due to time and budget constraints and was not intended in any way to be a scientific analysis. It nevertheless yielded a number of fascinating insights.

Broadly speaking, most of those interviewed had avidly followed the Hissène Habré trial on TV and in the press, had an impressive knowledge of the court and its process, and felt satisfied with the EAC and the verdict. From my small sample I was impressed at the eloquence and confident opinions expressed by ordinary people. A very typical comment was from Christian Mbaidoum, a teacher: 'It really made me proud, not just me but for the victims and all of Africa. To see a man who had done so much damage in the dock, his head bowed, not even able to speak, it is a very clear and healing signal'. A similar view was expressed by Bany Gonzemai, a young businessman: 'I think that the judgment can show that no one is untouchable; that everyone can expect to be judged for their actions one day'. 'It sends a message to other African leaders that bad political leadership could lead to a similar trial in the future', said student Gertrude Dany.

Questions unanswered

Despite the EAC's obvious success in convicting Habré, victims and many of those interviewed on the streets of N'Djamena by Augustin Zuzanne mentioned a number of issues surrounding the so-called 'completeness' of the verdict. The most important unfinished business for ordinary Chadians appears to have been the failure to extradite Habré's five alleged accomplices – Guihini Korei, Saleh Younouss, Abakar Torbo Rahama, Mahamat Djibrine and Zakaria Berdei – to stand trial alongside the former president. For many there is a sense that without their testimony, the full truth will never come out. It's important to recall that under Article 3 of the Chambers' statute, the EAC can prosecute 'the person or persons most responsible' for international crimes committed in Chad during the period 7 June 1982 to 1 December 1990, but the conviction and life sentences for Djibrine and Younouss in N'Djamena in late 2014 put an end to the hope that these two key figures would answer for their crimes in Dakar after Chad refused to extradite them (see Chapter 2). The whereabouts of the other three, Guihini Korei, Zakaria Berdei and Abakar Torbo Rahama, is still officially unknown. Although Habré would almost certainly have been convicted on command responsibility alone, the fact that the other five were not investigated by the court has left lingering questions from the ordinary Chadians interviewed for the survey about who was really in charge and the personal liability of those who actually carried out the torture. For example, Modou Ousmane, a public works engineer commented 'If the other DDS agents had been at the trial this would have influenced the verdict. I think the fact that they weren't there was perhaps the reason he refused to talk'. Christian Mbaidoum noted that 'He didn't kill on his own, he didn't torture on his own, he didn't cut people's throats on his own'. Not only Habré

Many have questioned why the EAC did not make more effort to secure the transferral of the five others accused, particularly after former Chadian Minister of Justice Jean-Bernard Padaré's claims (see Chapter 2) that he was on the verge of signing an agreement to transfer Younouss and Djibrine to Senegal after the N'Djamena trial, but that he received a mystery phone call from a high level in the Chadian administration telling him to cancel it. 'It left me with a really bad feeling', said Jacqueline Kounou, a fish seller working in the Kousseri neighbourhood. 'The other DDS agents are still at liberty in Chad and that means we will always be frightened of them.' 'People should be made to pay for their crimes', said Maimonne Jacque.

As we have seen in Chapter 3, there was a growing sense as the case progressed that the Chadian authorities were beginning to become uncomfortable with its increasing reach, with consistent rumours of concern at the highest level that the investigations might uncover evidence of the involvement in Habré's crimes by others still at liberty in Chad today. These suspicions rest mainly on the fact of the 'hasty' trial of the twenty or so former DDS agents who were jailed in N'Djamena just two months before the EAC opened its doors. Chad refused to let these convicted people travel to Dakar or to take part in the trial via video link. Some also suspect that the Chadian state's application to register as a civil party at the EAC, citing economic, financial and moral suffering when the ex-president fled to Senegal in 1990, was motivated by a desire to access documents available to the court.[2] This application was turned down by the EAC lawyers at the beginning of the trial. Even after the success of the first four *commissions rogatoires* which carried out fact-finding missions to Chad in 2013–14, a fifth was mysteriously cancelled. Some speculated that Mbacké Fall had expressed an interest in interviewing Younouss and Djibrine in jail and this had caused concern that they might have dangerous insider knowledge.[3]

Perhaps most controversially, over the years rumours have circulated that Chad's current President Idriss Déby Itno was himself involved in human rights abuses. Although Déby was seen by many as a hero for his decision to go into rebellion with Hassan Djamous in 1989, and has been celebrated as the man who toppled Habré, opened the DDS prisons in 1990s and put an end to the worst of the human rights abuses, Chadians with long memories have not forgotten that for most of the 1980s Déby served loyally under the former president. After impressive military campaigns in the late 1970s and early 1980s which caught the equally battle-savvy Habré's attention, Déby was made a general and commander in chief of the army from February 1983 to November 1985. He played a leading role commanding the FANT alongside Hassan Djamous against the Libyan aggression in the east in 1984, and again in 1987 during the 'Toyota war' phase and later became a military advisor to the president.

There has also been a long-standing lack of clarity over the role of the army and its command structure during Black September 1984. Habré's court-appointed defence team tried to suggest during the EAC hearings that in fact there was a question over the former president's whereabouts during the infamous Deli Farm massacre allegedly carried out by the FANT in September 1984. The defence claimed that Habré was on the Hajj in Mecca when it happened, making it all but impossible in an era before mobile phones for him to have personally ordered the attack. In trying to establish the truth of this claim, the EAC did its best to meticulously piece together the exact chain of events that led to Black September, using documents from the 1992 Truth Commission, evidence from Amnesty International and a number of witness statements. It concluded that preceding the campaign of repression, Habré had despatched a number of political envoys to the south throughout 1983 to negotiate with the leadership of the Codos rebels. These political missions had had some success in drawing up agreements to disarm the rebels and reintegrate them into the national army. However, on the eve of the final signing of the reintegration accords in August 1984, a number of Codos rebels deserted their camps and disappeared back into the bush to again take up arms, and led a number of deadly ambushes against the FANT. The EAC concluded from numerous witness testimonies that a presidential delegation which included Habré himself had indeed visited the south at some point later in September. This suggests the former president had been present for at least some of the repression.[4]

The Deli Farm massacre, in which over 200 people are believed to have died, appears to have taken place on 17 September. The EAC eventually established that the dates Habré travelled to Mecca were in fact 29 August to 9 September, showing clearly that he would have been able to order the Deli Farm attack himself.[5] So far, no evidence has emerged linking Déby to any of the crimes which happened during the worst periods of Black September. It is vital to remember that he was not indicted by the EAC. In addition, as the EAC concluded, Habré himself was considered as 'commander in chief' of the armed forces in his role as head of state, making him ultimately responsible for the behaviour of the armed forces – including any of its commanders – and was subsequently convicted under the provisions of the legal concept of 'command responsibility'.

Habré's stubborn decision to remain silent from the day of his arrest has also angered many and deprived victims of an explanation for the human rights abuses carried out during the 1980s. It has even been suggested that there was a pact of silence between the former president and the former DDS operatives convicted in N'Djamena in March 2015, who also refused to speak or to shed any light on their relationships and the mechanisms of the DDS. 'So many things should have come out at the trial. So many truths, but unfortunately that's just Africa', said Masna Gaston, a retired civil servant, in response to one of my survey questions. 'In my opinion the failure of the trial to get Habré to speak means it was a failure', argued Youssouf Ahmid, a telephone salesman in N'Djamena, 'This is the only international trial I've heard of where the accused did not speak.'

Many of the victims also return again and again to this question. I asked if they feel frustrated that they never got the chance to hear how he feels about his period in office and that he never offered any explanation. I asked if they think it was a deliberate strategy to derail the court process and to get the case against him dropped. Almost everyone I interviewed disagreed with this explanation. 'It was because he knew what he had done', said victim Paulette Ngak-outou, whose father, a policeman in Sarh, disappeared in 1984 and was never seen again. 'If he hadn't done it he would have tried to deny it. He would have defended himself. There was nothing he could say. Maybe if he'd explained something I would have been able to consider forgiveness, but now it's too hard to forgive him.'

'I was angry that he didn't speak. It was disrespectful to those who had suffered. I wanted to know how he could do this to other human beings', said Masme Menal Elisabeth, who suffered sexual violence and abuse at the Kalaite prison when she was just fifteen and still a virgin. 'But he knew what he did. He had no response. What could he say to defend himself? Nothing.'

'I think he was ashamed to talk', reflected Naomi Minguebeye. 'He couldn't accept what he had done so he just stayed silent.'

'I'm not bothered about his excuses … If he had tried to defend himself I wouldn't have cared', said Hawa Guankargue. 'I just still wonder what happened to my brother. But now I've got no hope. I will never know what happened to him and I'll never be able to say goodbye to him.'

'By staying silent he accepts his fate. A stronger man would have stood up and admitted when he had erred', concluded Ousmane Abakar Tahir, who spent four and half years as a prisoner of war after fighting with the GUNT at Faya Largeau in 1983.

There are also a number of unanswered questions from the trial itself which were not fully investigated mostly due to time and budget constraints. Notably there is the thorny issue of the lack of clarity over the exact number of victims. HRW's Olivier Bercault confirmed to the EAC during his testimony that the secret DDS communications uncovered in the organisation's headquarters in 2000 revealed the names of 1208 people who were killed or died in detention and 12,321 victims of torture, arbitrary detention and other human rights violations. While at the other end of the spectrum the head of the 1992 Truth Commission Mahamat Hassan Abakar testified at the EAC that his team's calculations had estimated at least 40,000 victims (these calculations were based on the fact that he had interviewed 4000 victims and assumed that he had only been able to reach 10% of the total number of victims). While the 40,000 figure seems to have been thrown into doubt by the trial, Mahamat Hassan Abakar staunchly stands by his calculations. This focus on the number of victims may seem like splitting hairs, but it is important to give a true picture of how human rights abuses committed in the 1980s in Chad can be compared to other traumatic events in other countries – particularly when civil party lawyers at the EAC compared Habré to Hitler and Chad to Rwanda on more than one occasion.

There were also some important lines of evidence which were not pursued at the trial. For example, there was disappointment that Gali Gatta Ngothe, a former special advisor to Habré who later joined the Hadjerai rebellion, touted as one of the 'star witnesses' in the case, never travelled to Dakar for the trial. Ngothe, who had previously spoken at length to investigators about Habré's working habits, attention to detail and refusal to tolerate insubordination, also mentioned the existence of a shady so-called 'parallel cabinet' made up of Anakaza Goranes (Habré's ethnic group). He alleged that during his own interrogation by the DDS after he had fallen foul of the system during the rebellion, he had heard the voice of the president over a walkie-talkie giving instructions to the interrogator.[6] 'It was a big disappointment that he did not testify', said HRW's Henri Thulliez, who felt that Ngothe's evidence could have shed light on the inner workings of the DDS.

At the same time the EAC failed to shed any light on the wider international political context of the 1980s, in particular the extent to which Habré and the DDS were aided and even encouraged by international powers. As we have seen in Chapter 1, groundbreaking research by HRW published just after the verdict in June 2016 showed the extent to which Habré's government had been supported financially and militarily by the Reagan administration in the US in the 1980s, and to a lesser extent by France. Documents collected by the 1992 Commission of Enquiry revealed direct financial support to the DDS from the US and reports of US 'special advisors' being present at the DDS headquarters. However none of this evidence was brought before the EAC, with the February 2013 indictment and the EAC founding statute both avoiding the question entirely. Nor was there was any mention of the political context of the 1980s in the 680-page full written judgment, which went into incredible levels of detail in establishing the background to many of the crimes committed under Habré. Only one witness mentioned the US support of Habré in the witness box in Dakar. As with other similar situations around the world where dictators are allowed by tacit consent from international powers to continue abusing their people, Habré's apparent confidence that he had powerful backers continues to frustrate the lawyer for the civil parties, Jacqueline Moudeina: 'Habré did not act alone. His silence was not free. He was covering for the US and France. He had a pact. The EAC was just not strong enough to face this issue.'[7]

At the opening of the EAC in July 2015 I couldn't help feeling a sense of irony at the appearance of Stephen Rapp, former ambassador-at-large and head of the Office of Global Criminal Justice in the US State Department. Visiting the trial as an observer, he was keen to see how the trial could offer opportunities to develop the justice systems in Senegal and Chad, as well as its potential for offering a new model of justice in other African conflicts including South Sudan.[8] When I spoke to him on the phone following the opening of the trial he made no mention of the close historical relationship between the US and Habré. I asked him about the involvement of the CIA, and the US's role in supporting Habré's regime, but he argued that it was not an important issue. Similarly, given how involved France continues to be in many of its former colonies including Chad, the French presence was conspicuously absent. The only French faces were Habré's advocate François Serres and lawyer William Bourdon, who acted for the civil parties.

This glaring missed opportunity by the court to shed light on how Habré was 'enabled' by foreign powers, and perhaps to warn against a similar situation occurring in the future, has not gone unnoticed in Chad. The issue came up on several occasions during conversations with former victims and observers during my last visit to Chad in January 2017. Ordinary Chadians also expressed disappointment when responding to my survey questions: 'These states gave Habré his zeal, their responsibility is clear', claimed Mahamat Moustapha Kochi. Koyasta Adeline, a teacher, said: 'France and the US cannot possibly say to us today that they didn't know what was going on at the time'. And at a debate in London during a screening of Mahamat-Saleh Haroun's film in late 2016, a student asked whether France and the US had a moral obligation to be the main contributors to the so-far empty Trust Fund for victims' compensation which was mandated by the founding statute.[9] Others, including University of Berkeley's Kim Thuy Seelinger who worked on the amicus brief for the victims of sexual violence, have voiced similar opinions.

However, it appears that a full exposé of international involvement was simply considered to be impractical for the EAC operating on a tight budget and schedule. In deciding to publish their report 'Enabling a Dictator' after the trial concluded in 2016, HRW seems to have decided to focus their attention during the trial phase on the more achievable goal of securing the conviction of the man considered to be at the heart of the operation. 'Superpower support just wasn't considered important enough', said Reed Brody. 'This was a trial of Hissène Habré, not the US. Perhaps if he had spoken and tried to defend himself it would have come up, but there just wasn't time or inclination to look into it.'[10] It is interesting to speculate why Habré declined the opportunity to lambast the role of France and the US in creating a permissive environment for the abuses to take place; perhaps because it undermined his criticism of the court as an 'imperialist' institution. What the US feels about its responsibility to Chad is a question which is now likely to be swept away with the passing of time and the arrival of Donald Trump in the Oval Office, a figure with no obvious interest in Africa let alone the details of US foreign policy thirty years ago. *Dig at Trump*

Impact of a court-appointed defence

It is likely we will never know what was going through Hissène Habré's mind when he made the crucial decision to remain silent during the trial. Nearly two years into his life sentence and with the failed appeal behind him, he has still refused to utter a word about his views on the trial or to shed any light on the political thinking behind Chad's years of repression. After several complex attempts to disrupt the establishment of the EAC at the ECOWAS court in 2014, it is interesting to speculate why Habré's French lawyer, François Serres, went on to conclude that it was in his client's best interest that he should be almost entirely absent from

The lawyer (French)

the EAC process in Dakar. Serres has in the past been known for a style known as 'théorie de la rupture' popularised by French lawyer Jacques Verges in his defence of Algerian militants, which aimed to discredit processes instituted by former colonial powers. Habré's decision to denounce the 'Imperialists' at the beginning of his trial could be seen as evidence of this. While for many of the victims, the silence was a clear admission of guilt and a recognition that what he had done was indefensible, it seems more plausible to see his refusal to cooperate with his court-appointed defence as designed to obstruct and hopefully derail the trial. Speaking to *Le Monde* in the days following the initial opening of the EAC in September 2015, Serres said that his strategy was a 'defence of refusal', calling the trial 'a farce' and Habré 'a scapegoat'.[11] He then stopped speaking about the case, but it is not known if he continued to advise Habré in private. The decision not to cooperate was bold, but its consequences turned out to be dire. He was left with a team of three Senegalese lawyers – Maitres Mbaye Sène, Abdou Gning and Mounir Ballal – who lacked a profound knowledge of politics and ethnic relationships in Chad, who struggled to communicate with the accused and had only limited time to prepare their defence.

It is important to note that the three defence lawyers were given an almost impossible task, but the inadequacy of the defence has left a number of lingering doubts and questions about the day-to-day mechanics of the abuses. The defence team chose not to focus on challenging Habré's guilt under command responsibility, although according to Emmanuelle Marchand, a lawyer who worked with Alain Werner to prepare the representation of the civil parties, there were a number of technical points they could have raised and challenged. The fact that they chose the case of the Ngalo massacre to prove that he had tried to stop abuses by the FANT was rather ironic since they appeared to happily accept that this meant he had also ordered the killing of the soldiers responsible. Rather than challenging technical details, the main

The defence's point of objection

strategy of the defence was to construct a rhetorical argument to try to undermine the assertion that Habré had known everything that was going on all the time, and to argue that there existed little proof of him personally committing crimes. The team repeatedly tried to assert that the DDS had actually been under the control of the then Minister of the Interior. In particular they tried to argue that Habré had been on the Hajj in Mecca during one of the worst periods of repression against the south during Black September 1984, and could not personally have given the orders for the massacre of Codos rebels at Deli farm (a theory which was discredited by the EAC). More broadly, they attempted to paint a picture of a 'patriot' who had defended Chad against the invading Libyan army at a time of existential crisis, and that the only victims had been insurgents.[12] They claimed that he had become the victim of a concerted political campaign started by groups such as Amnesty International with the complicity of the 1992 Truth Commission which had then been continued by the current Chadian government and HRW.

As we have seen, the defence also chose to go after a number of key witnesses to attempt to undermine their credibility. In particular they targeted the head of the Chadian Truth Commission Mahamat Hassan Abakar, alleging that he had been too close to President Déby when he had collected his evidence; they accused him of not being impartial and claimed that he had only gathered the testimonies of DDS agents who had been 'rehabilitated' under the new regime.[13] They also questioned the testimony of the key witness Khadidja Hassan Zidane who had alleged that Habré himself had raped her. They appeared to pour scorn on her decision not to reveal the rape at any point before the trial began, and pointed to the fact that there were no other witnesses to the alleged crime. Ballal seemed incredulous that she could not remember precise dates, including her own birth date. At one point they made the offensive comment that a president could not have been sexually interested in a woman who didn't wash.[14] After 'the official website of president Hissène Habré' had attempted to trash Zidane's testimony by calling her a 'crazy whore' and 'nymphomaniac prostitute',[15] and she and other female witnesses had been heckled by Habré's wife and supporters outside the courtroom, this regressive comment was perhaps expected to her. The defence asked the EAC to grant a medical examination of the scars that she had claimed to have received when the former president stabbed her in the leg, but this request was turned down. Other witnesses were challenged, including traditional chief and former minister Facho Balaam, who was cross-examined on the basis of having accepted to work for the Chadian state whilst simultaneously attempting to arrange secret meetings with Qaddafi's representatives.

These cross-examinations at times seemed uncomfortable to the court, but showed that the defence was doing its best to challenge the prosecution's case. However, it highlighted the fact that they lacked facts and documentary evidence of Habré's innocence, or indeed any information about the roles of the other five co-accused and other DDS agents incarcerated in Chad. Without a full understanding of the power structure in Chad in the 1980s, and only forty-five days to prepare when the human rights groups had been working on the case for twenty-five years, it was difficult for them to move beyond picking holes and apparent inconsistencies in individual accounts of events that took place more than thirty years before. More fundamentally, it showed how difficult it was to defend a man who refused to speak to them and apparently did not want to be defended. 'It was an impossible job', said Reed Brody, who believes that that the court-appointed defence team relied too heavily on an old line of Habré's own lawyers that any attempts to prosecute him were part of a political conspiracy between Chad's new government and international organisations. 'They could not move any further than the suggestion that Amnesty and the Truth Commission had started a lie in the 1990s which was still going.'

Defense lawyers ill-prepared — not their fault

The importance of outreach

As international justice has developed over the last twenty years, there has been an increasing amount of focus on the importance of community 'buy-in' and support for court processes. Part of the criticism levelled at the international ad hoc trials of the early 1990s, such as the ICTY and the ICTR, was that they were perceived to have failed in connecting the people affected by the atrocities with the trials which were carried out in their names. These trials were often carried out far from the scene of the alleged crimes and '[were] considered to lack legitimacy because those who have been most directly affected by the crimes lack "ownership" of the trials'.[16] Following on from those observations, the idea of building 'outreach' or sensitisation programmes into the work of special courts began in earnest at the 'next generation' of hybrid trials, the SCSL which opened in 2002, and the ECCC which opened in 2004. Academic Jane Stromseth from Georgetown University argues that the hybrids had a lot of work to do in this area. She paints a colourful metaphor:

> International and hybrid criminal trial may simply be a 'space-ship' phenomenon; they arrive, do their business and take off, leaving a befuddled domestic population scratching their heads and wondering what, if anything, this had to do with the dire realities on the ground … [which] include desperately under-resourced national judiciaries, limited public awareness or dissemination of laws, a dearth of capable judges, police, prosecutors or defence attorneys.[17]

The outreach programme for the SCSL has been described as 'far more extensive and ambitious than anything which has previously been undertaken',[18] and aimed to link the people of Sierra Leone with the court through disseminating information and encouraging serious dialogue and two-way communication.

It involved a series of innovative 'Town Hall Meetings' where the court's Registrar and Chief Prosecutor David Crane travelled to remote communities to meet ordinary people and discuss the court's work before it was officially inaugurated, as well as radio and TV spots, schools programmes and training workshops. Although this programme was hindered by lack of funding and the difficulties of travelling around Sierra Leone and communicating with large numbers of people with only basic schooling, it has been credited with disseminating basic information about the court and spreading the message that the court was 'aimed at ending impunity'.[19] One report found that 96% of people interviewed had at least heard of the trial. Nevertheless, several reports examining the effectiveness of the outreach programmes suggested that detailed knowledge of the court's inner workings was generally thin, and complex, negative and sometimes contradictory opinions were often held by research participants.

Several years later the ECCC began a programme of media sensitisation, including the production of radio and TV spots, and the organisation of community debates and training for specific groups such as lawyers and young people. Over 150,000 people visited the court between 2009 and 2014, and there was an extra focus on documenting people's experiences under the Khmer Rouge and giving advice to people wishing to form civil parties to participate in the trial. The ECCC sparked a lot of early interest from the public, particularly the first high-profile case of Comrade Duch, who had been in charge of a notorious prison camp. His case involved testimony about the shocking conditions in the prison; it was followed avidly across the country and he was eventually sentenced to life imprisonment. However, interest seems to have begun to wane as further cases were brought – the outreach programme suffered from a significant lack of funding, and unclear divisions of responsibilities between the international and Cambodian participants in the court, a function of its 'hybrid' status, which led to 'confusion and inefficiency'.[20] It was also hampered by difficulties in reaching remote, isolated rural communities, and the problems of illiteracy and lack of access to the internet. Many people were also suspicious of official government media and seemed to fear that the court was also propaganda. Ten years after it opened, research by the Open Society Justice Initiative (OSJI) suggested that support for the court had diminished and ordinary people were feeling that they lacked knowledge of the main cases before the ECCC;[21] the OSJI recommended that the outreach efforts of the court should be stepped up.

While the hybrids have made some progress, the ICC has also been limited in the amount of outreach and sensitisation it has been able to do. In 2013, Herman von Hebel, the court's Registrar, told the International Justice Monitor that 'we are not in a position to even come close to the amount of outreach and communication that the Special Court [for Sierra Leone] was able to do',[22] acknowledging the difficulties faced by an institution based in The Hague in Europe, on a limited budget with numerous cases in different locations to investigate at any one time. According to Phil Clark, there was no one on the ground to run an outreach programme for the first three years of the investigation in Uganda.[23] Even the ICC's own 2016 report examining how the court's Registry could be reorganised recognised a lack of on-the-ground presence in affected communities and that overall 'the outreach function [is] insufficiently developed'.[24] In addition, although there were early encouraging signs that victim participation was to be welcomed at the ICC, as time wore on it became more and more difficult to facilitate. It was expensive to help large numbers of victims to travel to The Hague, and their participation was seen in some quarters as unwieldy and hard to manage. Although in the early days victims were allowed to take part, the ICC was eventually obliged to narrow their role and create a 'common legal counsel' who was to become a focal point and would liaise with all the affected communities to represent their interests through a single unified voice. The effect, as Phil Clark explains, was that 'Victim participation became homogenised and sanitised'. Yet again, justice was veering back towards a distant concept carried out in European courtrooms.

The EAC's record

need for trial to be held in country

Although it has been broadly established that the EAC had value because it was an African court on African soil, for some Chadians at least the 'spaceship' phenomenon described by Stromseth still applies because the case took place in Senegal, a more developed country which is actually thousands of kilometres away. Some of those involved with the case bemoaned the general lack of cultural knowledge about Chad in Senegal.[25] 'The trial should have taken place in Chad, because that was where things happened', said Guerende Ngue in response to a survey question. 'The trial felt like it had nothing to do with our own judicial system, there was no positive impact, because it took place thousands of kilometres away', said Mahamat Moustapha, a retired civil servant.

Nevertheless, despite some disconnection with Chadians because of the EAC's location, it had some very real success in the field of outreach. From the start there was a commitment to ensuring that the Habré trial was broadly understood by Chadians and that justice should be more visible and relevant to the affected communities – in other words, not only should justice be done but it should be seen to be done. As an acknowledgement of the problems associated with holding the trial in Senegal and not in Chad itself, the founding statute of the EAC made allowances for the provision of 'conducting awareness activities and for informing both the African and international public on the work of the EAC'.[26] A very significant 10% of the total budget for the EAC was dedicated to outreach.[27] The statute also stated explicitly that open access should be provided for all concerned parties, including journalists, observers and members of civil society, and that the entirety of the proceedings should be video-recorded. It was indeed very easy to attend the trial and to follow every minute detail online. In addition, the EAC got off to an impressive start in developing its relationship with Chad, during the four investigation missions led by the Senegalese Chief Prosecutor Mbacké Fall (examined in Chapter 2). These visits were well-attended by Chadians and discussed widely in the local media, and appear to have gone a long way towards giving ordinary people a voice and helping them to see that the court was a serious process. But the court really does seem to have wanted to go further to ensure that the trial involved those physically unable to get to the court in Dakar mostly for reasons of poverty and lack of mobility.

The EAC Outreach Consortium was set up in 2014. For the first time the idea of outreach was clearly distinguished from the official communications service of the EAC which was attached to the courtroom in Dakar. The Outreach Consortium is in fact an independent body; the contract to run the operations was won by a consortium of three companies – Senegalese communications company Primum Africa Consulting; the Chadian communications company Magi Communications, run by civil society activist Gilbert Maoundonodji, who has campaigned tirelessly for transparency in Chad's extractives industry; and the Belgian NGO 'RCN Justice et Démocratie', which was created after the Rwandan genocide. 'This was actually very cost effective and allowed us to go further', said Franck Petit, a communications specialist working with the Consortium. 'It helped us to get started quicker and allowed us to target activities because our team already knew the ground so well. For example it was easy to find reliable partners in radio stations and theatre companies. It gave us credibility and independence because we weren't perceived to just be the mouthpiece of the court.'[28]

The Consortium has carried out numerous activities. Its main focus was on training around twenty Chadian journalists on the mechanics of the trial, and working with TV and radio companies in Chad to produce 'spots', discussion programmes and phone-ins which aimed to explain the proceedings, the charges and the court institutions to audiences. There was also specific focus on exploring what impact that EAC might have on international justice. The twelve introductory programmes were made in French, Sarha (one of the southern languages) and Chadian Arabic, and were produced by journalists from Radio Liberté FM in N'Djamena and Radio Kar Uba in Moundou, and then shared with a network of twelve partner community radio stations. Although it's notoriously difficult to get reliable listening statistics for Chadian radio stations, it is thought that these programmes could have been heard by thousands of people. The Consortium also set up a very useful website, the Inter-active Forum of the EAC,[29] which hosts discussion boards, forums and news updates from the trial. It also has a complete archive of all the court's proceedings including videos of each day's proceedings. Various booklets were produced to explain the founding statute of the EAC and the rights of the accused. There was also focus on training courses to help civil society activists understand the workings of the court in a bid to encourage victims and witnesses to come forward. The work of the Consortium has changed as the case has progressed: at first the focus was on establishing a national network of seven civil society coalitions to promote the work of the court across the country, whereas today the emphasis has shifted to explaining the verdict, the appeals process and how the compensation arrangements might play out.

Shift in focus

In addition, fifteen Chadian journalists were given financial assistance by the Consortium to travel to Dakar to cover six key moments in the trial and their reports were broadcast and published back home in Chad. Further grants were made available from the Open Society Initiative for West Africa, which contributed around $180,000. Even more interestingly, the Chadian state emerged as one of the major contributors to supporting press coverage of the trial, which seems to have been an indication that the authorities wanted to help ordinary Chadians to feel a sense of 'ownership' of the trial. A team of journalists from the Chadian Press Agency and state TV and radio (ONRTV) was despatched to Dakar for the whole trial and worked closely with the Senegalese national broadcaster RTS to set up a slightly delayed relay of the court proceedings which was shown on Chadian TV every day. Despite a few technical teething troubles at the beginning which were solved at the last minute by emergency funding from Senegal, almost all the EAC proceedings were streamed live on the internet, and almost all the sessions of the court have been posted to the Forum's You Tube channel. HRW commented that '[We] consider this a major success in ensuring that the trial was meaningful to, and understood by, the people of Chad and Senegal'.[30]

It was also good experience for some of the Chadian journalists I met in Senegal, who had imagined they would never be able to afford to travel to Dakar. 'It's been really interesting and important for us', Djimadoum Blaise, a reporter from the Chadian Press Agency, told me in Dakar in July 2015.[31] 'When I call home people tell me they've read my reports. They're really keen to know what's being said in court.'

The Consortium organised nearly fifty separate debates in Chad and Senegal, and twelve 'tournées' or outreach 'caravans' between January 2014 and January 2017, which visited fifteen towns across Chad and targeted about an estimated 25,000 people.[32] The caravans travelled to remote areas where open debates and question-and-answer sessions about the court proceedings were held in communities. The teams showed short video presentations of the highlights of the court case and invited guests to pose questions and speak to experts. For those involved in organising these caravans, debates and question-and-answer sessions, this was an interesting time to try to understand how ordinary people felt about the Habré story. It was not just a simple story of a victimised population being immediately grateful for the court's work. The EAC had its fair share of critics. A report from the Consortium visit to the southern town of Bongor in February 2016 is revealing in the kinds of questions and debates which came up. Necka Soua, a journalist from Radio Terre Nouvelle in Bongor, who had been fortunate enough to travel to Dakar to cover some of the proceedings, talked vividly about hearing the testimony of Khadidja Hassan Zidane who had accused the former president of raping her. He told the audience how Habré had been 'clearly embarrassed' and had shifted his feet and looked away as she spoke. This led to a fascinating debate about whether the 'man in the turban' who had hidden his face and refused to speak for six months was actually the former president and not an impostor, showing the level of distrust that some Chadians still hold towards the authorities. Other participants raised questions about why Habré had been able to keep his silence throughout the trial, and felt that the fact he had been carried into the court on the first day of proceedings was like 'being carried around like a hero'. Several people believed that the court was being too soft on the former president. A live debate held on local radio later that evening elicited questions about the type of sentence he was facing, and why he had not been tried in Chad. Another popular question was why current President Idriss Déby Itno had not been investigated on allegations of involvement in human rights abuses in the 1990s.[33] Another concern often raised at this public debate was the fact that Habré had been allowed to wear his turban and dark glasses for the entirety of the trial, something which many Chadians found to be disrespectful to the court. Others were frustrated at his refusal to ever address the court. In fact, these issues were addressed by presiding Judge Kam in his final judgment, where he acknowledged the 'insulting scorn' which Habré had shown towards the court, and this was taken into account in the final sentencing.

Impact on domestic justice systems

Previous hybrid and ad hoc trials have also tried to make a real and lasting impact on domestic justice systems. For example, the SCSL trained domestic police investigators, and the ICTR outreach programme in Rwanda placed computers in courthouses across the country. The EAC had no overt mandate to improve Chad's justice system, which was undoubtedly weak before the trial got underway.

egular reports of corruption in the judiciary, with bribes n commercial law cases and repeated allegations that the authorities interfere in court cases.[34] Courts are chaotic, lacking in resources, understaffed and regularly delayed – for example, in late 2016 all the country's magistrates went on a two-week strike over the non-payment of salaries. Little has changed in the day-to-day running of these bodies.

In terms of training domestic personnel, none of the prosecution team or judges in the Dakar case were Chadian, so it does not appear that the EAC has done much to influence the structure of the legal system from the inside. In fact, the issue elicited a number of spirited responses to my survey questions in N'Djamena. 'We mustn't kid ourselves. Every Chadian has lost confidence in the justice system because not all of those who were guilty of crimes in the 1980s have been jailed', said Djimnaren Edmond, an unemployed graduate. 'In fact things have got worse since the trial', noted another respondent. 'There are arbitrary arrests, crimes, kidnappings and intimidation against ordinary people in the street. The judges are corrupt and justice only comes to those higher up in the social order.' 'Citizens are persecuted by the judiciary for their opinions, others for political choices. Things today are worse than under Habré', commented another respondent.

However, it must be acknowledged that there has been an observable impact on the individual skills and confidence of the key players in the civil parties team. As we heard in Chapter 3, a number of prominent Chadian lawyers got the opportunity to represent the civil parties on an international stage, and to learn from the support and cooperation of a number of experienced lawyers such as Alain Werner and William Bourdon. Figures such as Jacqueline Moudeina, Delphine Djiraibe and Phillipe Houssine benefited from being able to stand up in front of an internationally credited tribunal and plead their case. 'It was an enormous learning experience for the Chadian teams', said Emmanuelle Marchand, who worked with Alain Werner. 'They learnt a lot about international law, different modes of liability such as command responsibility which don't exist in national law. It was a real exchange of knowledge.' Jacqueline Moudeina told me that she learnt huge amounts about international law through her participation in the case. Jean-Bernard Padaré, Chad's Justice Minister at the time of the Habré arrest and indictment, agreed: 'It has had a significant impact on our understanding of the role of justice. It's made us realise that courts can be independent and no one is above the law'.[35]

In addition, the picture gets more interesting if we examine the case of the twenty-three former DDS agents who were tried on charges of torture by the N'Djamena Criminal Court starting in November 2014. For a start this case was an enormous test for the N'Djamena court, in terms of both managing the caseload on a very tight timescale, and demonstrating political independence. At the beginning of the trial, Chief Prosecutor Rapambe Mahouli Bruno said that the case would allow 'the Chadian justice system to show its capacities' and respond to expectations of a fair hearing.[36] Despite a suspension in the middle of the case when a number of legal personnel went on strike over unpaid salaries, in general the court was able to hear from all witnesses and victims and conclude the case within a few months. Although it may be possible to speculate that the court had been given the green light from the powers that be in Chad to proceed in confidence, and perhaps even with a favoured outcome in mind, the Criminal Court nevertheless came out with a very significant judgment finding twenty of the accused guilty – people who had possibly rubbed shoulders with Déby when he was army chief of staff and who had been living at liberty for many years. The court confiscated the real estate and personal assets of those convicted and stripped them of any decorations, and most significantly it also held that the Chadian state was liable for the DDS agents' actions and ordered that the government should pay half of the $125 million in compensation which it awarded. While this did not imply that the court judged the current government to be ultimately responsible, it nevertheless demonstrated an encouraging tendency towards taking independent (and somewhat uncomfortable) judicial decisions.

There has been a much more visible impact on the Senegalese justice system, which has shown itself capable of effectively prosecuting serious international crimes. In order to give the Senegalese courts jurisdiction to try international crimes, the country's Code Pénale was amended on several occasions, including a new law which was passed in 2007 to allow the country to try crimes against humanity, war crimes and torture even when committed outside the country. There was also a constitutional amendment allowing possible cases to be tried retroactively and clarification on the implementation of the universal jurisdiction principle. This new framework creates enormous potential for Senegal to develop and expand its experience of trying international crimes in the future, helping it to live up to its ambitious aim to be a leader in African justice. 'For Senegal to keep this legislation on the books after the conclusion of the case is unusual and very significant', said Phil Clark.[37] And it's not just the legislation. As most of the judges and prosecution teams in the EAC were Senegalese, there has been a direct effect on these individuals' professional experience. Several of those who worked on the EAC have said their confidence has grown. Chief Prosecutor Mbacké Fall told me that he was delighted to have been involved: 'It made me realise I want to work on international law and gave me the confidence to submit a job application to the ICC, something I would never have thought about before'.[38] Although he didn't get the job, Fall said he is determined that he will be able to make something of the experience of working on the Habré case. Even if it is unlikely that a replica of the EAC will emerge in the immediate future, these personal successes show that a number of key individuals may now have the skills and confidence necessary to begin to influence domestic justice in their own countries, and possibly to take on further international cases in the future.

well this is patronizing.

Chapter 5

THE INTERNATIONAL CONTEXT

No sooner had the Habré verdict fallen than the excitement began to mount particularly among African observers that the EAC hybrid tribunal model could be a game-changer for African justice. 'This landmark decision should … provide impetus to the African Union or individual African states to replicate such efforts to deliver justice to victims in other countries in the continent', said Amnesty International's Gaetan Mootoo,[1] who worked on the Chad brief during the 1980s and early 1990s. A number of observers and editorials began to explore whether we might expect similar hybrid tribunals to be set up in Africa to try other cases of human rights abuses.[2]

Here was the very epitome of a lost cause, with a man who had evaded numerous attempts to bring him to justice for almost a quarter of a century; but it had been transformed through sheer persistence into a decisive judgment and conviction. Despite the former president's attempts to discredit and derail the process at the beginning, the EAC had surprised many by staying on track, on schedule and on budget. The whole case had been heard in ten months, and the total cost was about $9.5 million, a twelfth of the cost of a case at the International Criminal Court, according to Thierry Cruvellier.[3] It had been run by African judges and prosecutors, Chadian lawyers had pleaded on behalf of the civil parties and the courtroom had been based on African soil, and not in distant European courtrooms. There had been exciting developments in recognising rape and sexual violence as crimes against humanity, and victims and witnesses had played a crucial role in continuing the fight for justice and helping to build the prosecution case. 'Never before at the international level had victims' voices been so dominant', said journalist Thierry Cruvellier, who has written extensively about international justice and specifically the ECCC in Cambodia.[4]

Before analysing the potential role for hybrid tribunals, however, it is important to contextualise the EAC in terms of the wider experience of delivering justice in the African context. Part of the reason for the enthusiasm generated by the EAC experience is that the Habré trial happened at a time when the sense of disappointment with the ICC was mounting in Africa. After much initial optimism in the early 2000s that the ICC could become a powerful tool in helping end impunity and human rights abuses around the world, by the time the EAC opened in Dakar in 2015 the ICC had suffered a number of humiliating setbacks in its attempts to indict African leaders, and was on the verge of being rejected by several African states. While there is no suggestion that the technical negotiations to set up the EAC at the AU were carried out in reaction to the political difficulties with the ICC (the timing of the EAC was in fact merely a coincidence – as we heard in Chapter 2 it had been delayed and postponed many times, even as the ICC was initially looking to prosecute its first African subjects), it is nonetheless instructive to examine the court and to understand the challenges it has faced.

The establishment of the ICC

The Rome Statute creating the ICC was opened for signature and ratification in July 1998. The Court's norms have been described as 'idealistic',[5] and stemming from the emerging post-Second World War consensus on human rights in which the 1948 Nuremberg trials took place and concepts such as crimes against humanity and genocide were developed and clarified. Its direction and structure were also influenced by lessons from the experience of the ICTY (which closed its doors in 2017 after twenty-five years of operations) and the ICTR. Both of these institutions had ground-breaking successes – all of the targets of the ICTY either faced trial or died and the ICTR completed fifty prosecutions and convicted twenty-nine people. The ICTR also had the first-ever prosecution and conviction of a perpetrator of rape as genocide which has been key in the elevation of sexual violence as an international crime.

Nevertheless, the ICTY suffered from delays, lack of administrative support and lack of budget – even as the war and its associated crimes rumbled on. NATO and French forces based in the region seemed reluctant to arrest any suspected war crimes suspects, and two of the most feared leaders, Radovan Karadic and Ratko Mladic, remained on the run until 2008 and 2011 respectively. It led to calls that international prosecutions should be speeded up. The ICTR also came into conflict with the Rwandan authorities, led by the RPF of Paul Kagame, which had driven the fightback against the *genocidaires* in 1994 over issues of sovereignty, location (it was based in Arusha, Tanzania) and attempts to apply justice evenly to both sides in the conflict. For example, plans by the Chief Prosecutor Carla del Ponte to investigate an alleged RPF massacre of Hutu civilians in 1994 'provoked outrage and open defiance in Kigali'.[6]

Hybrid courts such as the SCSL and the ECCC were seen to some extent as a 'natural evolution of international criminal justice' and promised an alternative to purely domestic prosecutions, which were often politically impossible, without having to turn to big international trials. The ICTY and the ICTR had taken place at long distances from where the crimes were actually committed, and had been criticised for prioritising international prosecutors and judges over domestic personnel. This led some to conclude that the trials failed to help those affected by the crimes to feel a sense of 'ownership' of the justice. Hybrid trials, on the other hand, were thought to offer the potential for a positive 'trickle-down' effect on national norms of justice, as international lawyers worked alongside national lawyers. It was also thought that this would allow local people to feel more closely connected to the justice that was being carried out in their names. 'It was widely believed that the hybrid tribunals could leave a legacy of holistic rule of law reform ... above and beyond the broad sociological impact of trials', says academic Padraig McAuliffe.[7] However, as the 2000s progressed, hybrid trials dwindled in popularity as the ICC began to assume its full powers. They were dismissed by some for their 'perceived betrayal of earlier hopes'.[8] In addition, they were criticised for political bias and interference at the domestic level, and in some cases were unable to prosecute or make significant progress.

As international justice developed during the 1990s and 2000s, the ICC had been conceived as a *permanent* institution which would replace the 'ad hoc' and hybrid trials that had all been set up from scratch to deal with individual cases of human rights abuses. It has been described as 'the logical and almost natural next step',[9] offering the means to deal with abuses almost as they happened, to act as a deterrent, and to improve on the hybrid trials which had been criticised for promising too much while being unable to withstand domestic political intimidation. In the early years of the ICC's operation it was widely assumed that the hybrid model blending domestic and international elements would cease to be relevant, because the ICC would only intervene in cases where domestic judiciaries were incapable of holding their own trials (the so-called 'complementarity principle').

The founding documents of the ICC sought to direct the court away from the more 'common-law blueprints of adversarial proceedings mediated by neutral, "referee" judges' toward the tradition of civil law, with an emphasis on creating a more victim-focused 'restorative' justice.[10] Reparations or compensation would become central through the establishment of novel 'Trust Funds' for victims, building on the 'old' approaches of simply prosecuting offenders and jailing them.[11] Victims were given a higher profile in cases through the encouragement of the participation of civil parties (see Chapter 2). Systems were put in place to regularise funding and to limit the length of cases and appeals.

The Rome Statute came into force on 1 July 2002 when the necessary number of signatures had been acquired, much sooner than many had expected. Most of the early signatories were European states and smaller countries in Latin America and Africa under an umbrella of a supportive 'like-minded group' (LMG). Four of the five permanent members of the UN Security Council, however, were not overtly supportive of the court, with only the UK joining the LMG group. China, Russia and India did not sign, and in fact when the ICC first began its work more than two-thirds of the world's population was outside its jurisdiction. One of the biggest early critics of the court was the US, which was uncomfortable with the ICC's perceived threat to national sovereignty and the possibility that US officials could be summoned before it. Although Bill Clinton had signalled a more favourable attitude and had signed but not ratified the Rome Statute, when George W. Bush assumed the presidency his administration, particularly John Bolton, became vocal opponents. In the post-9/11 era, where certain torture methods had been approved by the US authorities and the question of the legality of the US/UK invasion of Iraq in 2003 had caused such international tensions, the court's potential jurisdiction appeared to be a major threat. However the ICC's behaviour during the 2000s appears to have slowly reassured the US that it would not become an overt target – the institution did not seem keen to open an investigation into the Iraq or Afghanistan wars (the US was not a member so did not fall under its jurisdiction in any case) and as we shall see, its early targets in Africa (for example the LRA) in fact often mirrored US foreign policy objectives. By the time Barack Obama took over in 1998, the US attitude to the court had become much more favourable. 'There is strong circumstantial evidence that the court has used its discretion in opening investigations to avoid entanglement with major powers and to re-assure ut the court's intentions', argues author David Bosco. 'The prosecutor's signals to the US on Iraq in 2003 were early evidence of this trend'.[12]

The ICC and Africa

Many African nations were initially supportive of the idea of a universal court as a way to combat impunity and human rights abuses on the continent. This was evidenced through initiatives such as the 1998 Dakar Declaration from twenty-five African countries that called for an independent and effective international criminal court to be established, and the participation of many African countries in the initial talks leading up to the creation of the Rome Statute. 'Africa's call for the establishment of the ICC came from the highest levels of the continent's leadership', argues academic Rowland J.V. Cole.[13] The African Commission on Human and Peoples' Rights called on African states to ratify the Rome Statute, and in fact Senegal was the first country to do so in February 1999. The court also gained much support from African NGOs and civil society groups acting on behalf of victims of human rights abuses. Thirty-four African countries became members of the ICC, and early developments seemed to suggest that the court could become a significant player on the continent.

DRC and Uganda

The first two cases the court examined were in Uganda and the DRC. In December 2003 Ugandan President Yoweri Museveni sent a letter to Luis Moreno-Ocampo, the ICC chief prosecutor, referring the situation in northern Uganda to the court. Led by Joseph Kony, a spiritual healer who emerged from a previous movement in the late 1980s in the Acholi region claiming that society had to be purified by violence, the Lord's Resistance Army has been attacking and terrorising the civilian population in northern Uganda and fighting the Ugandan government for many years.[14] Nominally motivated by Christianity, their tactics involve kidnapping children to become child fighters and girls to be sex slaves, attacking villages and massacring and mutilating their populations. Hundreds of thousands of people were forced into refugee camps in northern Uganda (a figure which reached 1.5 million people by 2004) due to the violence and insecurity. The Ugandan army's (UPDF, Ugandan People's Defence Force) fightback was hampered by the group crossing over borders into largely ungoverned territory in DRC and Sudan; in later years the group was even able to operate as far away as the forests of eastern CAR.

President Museveni at that time was still enjoying a reputation in the West as an independence hero who would do business with international powers, and Kony 'was as close as an individual could be to an international outcast'.[15] Following close cooperation between the chief prosecutor and the president, in July 2005 the ICC issued arrest warrants for Joseph Kony, his deputy Vincent Otti and three other senior LRA commanders including the former child soldier turned senior commander of the LRA, Dominic Ongwen. The investigation was unusual in that it was started before a true end to the fighting had been achieved, but this caused a backlash in Uganda, with the ICC becoming embroiled in complex debate about the relative importance of seeking peace versus seeking justice. Negotiators, including the indefatigable Betty Bigombe, who had been engaged with the rebels in the north of Uganda for several years and had begun to have some success with amnesty and ceasefire programmes for former fighters, worried that the move would lead to the breakdown of talks. 'The government's own Amnesty Commission expressed fears that the announcement by the ICC could make a peaceful resolution of the eighteen-year conflict impossible', according to Tim Allen.[16]

Kony duly disappeared back into the bush, announcing that he would resist arrest, and was reported to have entered the DRC. Vincent Otti was apparently killed by Kony, and the attacks on villages continued. In 2006 Kony told top UN diplomat Jan Egeland that he wanted the arrest warrants lifted as a precondition to rejoining peace talks. NGOs and human rights organisations began to criticise the ICC investigation and arrest warrants, with some pointing out that most of the rebel army were children; some feared that it would interrupt traditional justice systems and asked why alleged abuses by the UPDF were not being investigated. At the same time the ICC looked weak in its dealings with the government. Moreno-Ocampo's willingness to work with Museveni at the beginning had made many defenders of the court uncomfortable, but then the formerly supportive president appeared to have second thoughts about the ICC's involvement. For example, in 2004, when peace talks were back on track, he declared "the state could withdraw its case and we could inform the ICC that we have a solution to the Kony problem'.[17] The perceived threat of the ICC on Uganda's sovereign ability to solve the crisis became an issue; as Tim Allen has argued, 'It … seems unlikely that President Museveni would have initiated the prosecution if he thought he could not control it'.[18] Gradually the rhetoric became more embittered, with Museveni accusing the ICC of neo-colonialism and offering Kony and his associates immunity from prosecution. As Benjamin Schiff has argued, 'The Uganda referral appeared to be a great first opportunity … however the Office of the Prosecutor discovered escalating complexities'.[19] Slowly it became obvious that the ICC would struggle in Uganda. Today, twelve years after those arrest warrants were issued, only two of the original men indicted – Joseph Kony and Dominic Ongwen – are still alive. Dominic Ongwen went on trial in The Hague in late 2016 after handing himself over. His trial, a success in itself, has nevertheless raised complex problems as he has argued that as a former victim of child abduction himself, he is not liable for the crimes he has been accused of.[20] As for Joseph Kony, there have been a number of high-profile international initiatives to stop the LRA, including the controversial US-based 'Kony 2012' campaign, and a deployment of US Special Forces to the dense forests of CAR. At the time of writing he is still at large.

In April 2004 the Congolese government under Joseph Kabila asked the ICC to pursue investigations on its territory. Since 1996 the country had been wracked by a devastating civil war spawned by regional population movements following the Rwandan genocide and the disintegration of Mobutu Sese Seko's rule; the conflict had drawn in nine African countries and had caused the deaths of millions of its citizens. Although shaky truces had been signed, a number of anti-government militias continued to operate in the north-east of the country with the support of Rwanda and Uganda. Among these was the Union of Congolese Patriots led by Thomas Lubanga, in the restive province of Ituri. Like most militia commanders in the region, Lubanga had been accused of recruiting child soldiers and exactions against civilians, but his downfall began when his faction attacked a group of UN peacekeepers in February 2005 and killed nine Bangladeshis. When he was arrested and taken to Kinshasa, the ICC saw its chance. In early 2006 an arrest warrant was issued against him on charges of recruiting child soldiers. Kabila, whose 'willingness to engage international justice could improve his international standing', soon agreed to the transfer of Lubanga to The Hague.[21] He was to become the ICC's first suspect in detention, described as a historic turning point by Moreno-Ocampo.

However, this case also had problems. There were delays at the beginning of the trial, and even an attempt to get the charges annulled. Some critics complained that Lubanga was a relatively minor figure and that charges of recruiting child soldiers, although serious, were not of the magnitude that the ICC had been designed for. 'The court's selection of cases convinced some observers that the court had trimmed its investigations to suit regional and international political realities', says David Bosco.[22]

Nevertheless other notable successes followed. The court took custody of another suspect, Mathieu Ngudjolo Chui, another warlord from Ituri, and in 2008 it issued an arrest warrant for Bosco Ntaganda, whose forces had been able to run riot in eastern DRC for many years. A highly significant moment came in May 2008 when Belgian police arrested Jean-Pierre Bemba, a militia leader from the east who had come second in DRC's 2006 elections. He was transferred to The Hague on charges of committing war crimes in neighbouring CAR from 2002 to 2003, when his militia was asked by CAR's then president to help put down a rebellion. There was success on almost all of these fronts: Thomas Lubanga was finally convicted in March 2012 and sentenced to fourteen years in jail, and Bemba was convicted and jailed for eighteen years in 2016. In 2013 Bosco Ntaganda voluntarily walked into the US embassy in Rwanda asking to be transferred to the ICC and his trial began in September 2015. Only Mathieu Ngudjolo Chui was acquitted after the court found the prosecution had not proven his responsibility beyond all reasonable doubt.

Sudan

The tension between the ICC and African leaders began to ratchet up when it came to Darfur. In late 2003 the Sudanese government had begun to crack down hard on a number of rebel groups including the JEM (Justice and Equality Movement) led by Khalil Ibrahim and the SLM (Sudan Liberation Movement) led by Minni Minnawi, based in western Sudan in the three provinces of Darfur. Here a number of mostly non-Arabic-speaking African ethnic groups including the Fur, Massalit and Zaghawa resented the control of the Arabic-speaking elites of distant Khartoum. Drought, poverty and degradation of traditional herding lands had combined to create a dangerous sense of marginalisation. Their attacks on police and the military sparked a retaliatory 'scorched earth' campaign led by horse-riding 'Janjaweed', mostly Arab proxy militias, which killed thousands and drove hundreds of thousands of refugees over the border into eastern Chad. Thanks in part to a high-profile campaign led mostly by human rights activists in the US, the Darfur crisis soon hit the headlines.

At first the ICC did not take an active interest in the case. Sudan was not a signatory to the court and therefore it had no jurisdiction, failing a referral from the UN Security Council, which of course was heavily influenced by the less than enthusiastic US. However, as the desperate plight of the refugees in eastern Chad became public, and the reports began to emerge of mass killings, rape and pillage, momentum grew to classify the crisis as a genocide. Using this word very deliberately created an obligation on international players to act, and in March 2005 the UN Security Council voted to refer the situation to the ICC. The US tactfully decided to abstain from the vote rather than block it entirely, along with China, another major detractor of the court and a close ally of Sudan thanks to its oil projects based in the south. The referral seemed to be a game changer for the ICC's profile and influence, and 'appeared to transform the relationship between the superpower and the court ... at least the possibility to go towards a policy of benign neglect (from the United States)'.[23]

The court began an investigation in Sudan, but was hampered by its desire not to alienate the Sudanese government at an early stage. Investigators did not travel to Darfur but instead sought evidence among the displaced populations in eastern Chad's refugee camps. However, once the court had decided in early 2007 to issue arrest warrants for two individuals close to President Omar Al-Bashir on detailed charges of funding, organising and authorising attacks on the civilian population – Ali Kushayb, the leader of a Janjaweed militia, and Ahmed Haroun, a former Minister of the Interior – cooperation between the Sudanese authorities and the court broke down entirely. Khartoum began to frustrate the investigation and refused to hand over Ali Kushayb, who had briefly been in government custody. It made vocal proclamations denouncing the ICC's move and 'spontaneous' demonstrations against the court broke out in Khartoum and around the country. Yet again the court appeared to be at the centre of a complex international dialogue about bringing peace versus justice – with some international players feeling the unenforced arrest warrants merely provoked the Sudanese authorities. The casualties in Darfur continued to mount.

And then in July 2008 Luis Moreno-Ocampo dropped his bombshell. He announced that he was seeking an arrest warrant against the sitting Sudanese president Omar Al-Bashir for genocide, crimes against humanity and war crimes. He accused the president of having directed the policy of destroying ethnic groups based in Darfur. While the move was greeted with delight by many campaigners, there appeared to be some anxiety in the international community about the possible effects of antagonising the president: 'these conversations made clear that diplomats did not relish the idea of turning President Bashir into an international fugitive'.[24] The Khartoum government responded angrily to the threat of arrest and a number of international organisations withdrew their personnel from Sudan and Darfur as a precaution. Moreno-Ocampo was determined in the face of much international opposition, particularly from the AU which for the first time came out with an unsupportive view, claiming that the prosecutor was acting recklessly with the diplomatic process. There was even an unsuccessful attempt led by British and French diplomats to get the investigation into Al-Bashir deferred in return for Sudan allowing in peace-keeping troops.

The prosecutor hit back at criticism from the international community with accusations that the West was being weak on Al Bashir. In March 2009 the arrest warrant was finally issued on seven charges: five of crimes against humanity and two of war crimes (the genocide charge was issued on a second arrest warrant). 'Ocampo's argument was that ... as commander-in-chief at the apex of Sudan's military and political structure he was ultimately responsible for the slaughter'.[25] I was in eastern Chad visiting the Darfur refugee camps when the decision fell. I was inundated with excited calls from international news organisations which wanted to hear the reactions of the displaced people. Wandering round the wind-blown, dusty tents of the Goz Beida refugee camp with a microphone in hand, the reaction was mixed. While I did indeed find a few apparently spontaneous pro-ICC demonstrations, a UN flag waving from the top of one of the tents and several people expressing joy and a rather tragic optimism that they would soon be seeing the President, whom they blamed for all their troubles, in the dock at The Hague, a lot of people in the camps did not seem to show a great deal of emotion. While in Chad this was most likely due to the news simply not filtering through, over the border in Sudan there was outright fear. According to journalist Rob Crilly, who was in Darfur at the time, officials had warned the displaced people living in camps that they would have their hands cut off if they reacted to the news of the indictment. And as soon as the arrest warrant was announced, Sudanese officials made good on a threat to expel more than a dozen international humanitarian agencies working in Sudan and Darfur, with drastic consequences for those stuck in the camps, who were entirely dependent on them. 'The results were immediate. ... [Bashir] was turning the screw. Millions of people – families who had already lost their homes and faced a daily battle for survival – were much, much worse off', said Rob Crilly.[26]

Al Bashir seemed unfazed by the arrest warrant. Days later, he made a trip to Darfur itself in the presence of the international diplomatic corps, where he shook hands with ambassadors and promised peace; crowds turned out in front of the assembled journalists to denounce the ICC's move and to chant his praises. He appeared to feel confident enough in his position to begin to organise a number of foreign visits. According to the terms of the arrest warrant, any ICC member state had an obligation to arrest him if he arrived on their territory. His first trip was to Eritrea, followed by Egypt, in March 2009, but neither country had ratified the Rome Statute. He left both countries a free man.

In July 2010 he made a controversial trip to Chad, a signatory to the ICC. Chad's position regarding Sudan at that time was quite extraordinary. The two countries had long been allies due to their shared desert border and cultural, ethnic and linguistic links. However, Darfur had pushed that relationship to the limits. The

JEM's leader Khalil Ibrahim was a Zaghawa kinsman of Idriss Déby, who had come under enormous pressure from his ethnic group to turn a blind eye to the JEM's infiltration of refugee populations in eastern Chad and the establishment of rear bases. In retaliation, Sudan had begun to finance and arm a number of Chadian rebel groups, based in Darfur, which were able to launch lightning attacks on N'Djamena in 2006 and 2008 that came close to toppling Déby. Diplomatic relations between the two countries had repeatedly been cut off, and Chad agreed to allow an EU/UN peacekeeping mission (MINURCAT) to deploy on the border in 2008, which deeply antagonised Khartoum. Chad was suspected to have been behind a JEM attack on Omdurman in 2008. In 2008, when the ICC arrest warrant against Al Bashir was initially issued, Chad had been openly delighted as it had been struggling to deal with the influx of refugees as well as the proxy rebel war with Sudan. The country had indicated a willingness to arrest him, bringing it into conflict with the AU, which was intrinsically opposed to the idea of arresting sitting heads of state and had already criticised the prosecutor's move as jeopardising the peace process in Darfur. However, by 2010 the relationship between Chad and Sudan had been completely turned on its head. The two countries had almost miraculously agreed to put aside their differences in late 2009; Déby visited Khartoum and within weeks Déby had kicked out the UN mission MINURCAT, replacing it with a joint border force. When Al Bashir arrived in N'Djamena for a meeting of CENSAD (Community of Sahelian States) in July 2010, he was greeted like an old friend by Déby. After once seeming the most likely African candidate to betray Al-Bashir, Chad now flatly ignored every appeal from around the world to follow through on the arrest warrants.[27]

It was a precedent which was quickly followed by a number of provocative trips to Kenya, Djibouti and Malawi, all of them state parties of the ICC. By now it seemed that Al Bashir had become highly confident that he would not be arrested by any of his African allies. The inability of the ICC to enforce its arrest warrants was most dramatically highlighted by Al Bashir's visit to South Africa in 2015, where he attended an AU heads of state summit. This visit caused worldwide controversy, as South Africa had initially been one of the ICC's staunchest advocates. Despite a High Court order being issued for his arrest just hours before he was due to fly out of Johannesburg, the South African authorities allowed him to leave on the basis that as a head of state, Al Bashir had immunity from arrest.[28] Although the ICC had aimed extremely high in targeting Al Bashir, his untroubled peregrinations showed clearly how difficult it could be to enforce an arrest warrant. The sea change in some African countries' initial support of the institution was becoming painfully obvious.

Kenya

In March 2010 the ICC began an investigation into the violence which had racked Kenya following disputed presidential elections in December 2007. Supporters of opposition candidate Raila Odinga had taken to the streets to decry fraud, which led to rioting and clashes with supporters of incumbent president Mwai Kibaki. The situation rapidly descended into inter-ethnic killings, sexual violence, destruction of property and displacement. By the end of February 2008 it was estimated that 1200 people had died. In this case Kenya was a state party to the ICC, but until 2010 little progress had been made locally in prosecuting those believed to be behind the violence. Without a Security Council referral, Luis Moreno-Ocampo initiated the investigation himself using his *proprio motu* powers.[29] The investigation was quickly followed with summonses for six people: Deputy Prime Minister Uhuru Kenyatta, Cabinet Secretary Francis Muthaura and Police Commissioner Mohammed Hussein Ali on the side of Kibaki's Party of National Unity; and Education Minister William Ruto, Industry Minister Henry Kosgey, and radio host Joshua Arap Sang on the side of Raila Odinga's Orange Democratic Movement. The case was immediately controversial. Some welcomed the move, but others greeted it with shock. International observers questioned the repeated focus of the ICC on African cases when it had declined the opportunity to investigate two other conflicts of a similar magnitude which had broken out at around the same time as the Kenyan violence: the Russia/Georgia war of August 2008 and the Gaza War in late 2008.

At first the Kenya case got off to a reasonable start. All the suspects voluntarily travelled to The Hague in April and September 2011 to attend preliminary hearings. The Pre-Trial Chamber declined to confirm the charges against Ali and Kosgey in 2012, and those against Muthaura withdrawn in 2013, but the court pushed ahead with prosecutions of Ruto and Sang for crimes against humanity of murder, forcible transfer, and persecution, and Kenyatta for the crimes against humanity of murder, forcible transfer, rape, persecution and other inhumane acts.[30] The trial of Ruto and Sang began in September 2013, and Kenyatta's trial was scheduled to start in 2014.

However, the cracks soon started to appear. Starting from 2013 a number of the original witnesses in the case began to withdraw their testimonies. Allegations of bribery and intimidation against witnesses, including death threats and threats to burn down houses, began to emerge.[31] Some said they were too scared to appear. The chief prosecutor said that Kenya was not doing enough to protect witnesses,[32] but others claimed that the court itself should take more responsibility in this respect. An arrest warrant for three people accused of witness intimidation was not followed through by Kenya, and a further eight key witnesses pulled out in April 2014, undermining the prosecution case. An ICC report suggested that there had been a systematic campaign of intimidation and bribery.[33] Furthermore, there was some doubt about the reliability of a number of 'key' Mungiki witnesses who were central to the case.[34] Fatou Bensouda, who in 2012 had taken over from Luis Moreno-Ocampo, complained that the Kenyan government was refusing to cooperate or to hand over crucial evidence.

The witness problems were followed by an extraordinary run-in between justice and politics. In 2013, Kenyatta and Ruto – such bitter rivals in the 2007 election – teamed up to fight the presidential election under the banner of the Jubilee Coalition, again taking on Raila Odinga. They were able to successfully paint themselves as the victims of an international witch hunt and ramped up the anti-ICC rhetoric by highlighting its failure to prosecute anyone outside of Africa. On 9 March Kenyatta was announced the winner, with William Ruto becoming his deputy Prime Minister. Yet again, the ICC was faced with the dilemma of pursuing a case against an un-cooperative elected head of state. Kenyatta's case was due to start in The Hague in September 2014, but was delayed at the last minute after Bensouda asked for an adjournment as she had not been able to gather sufficient evidence to prove his guilt beyond all reasonable doubt.[35]

Finally the pressure on the ICC proved too much and the case against Kenyatta was dropped in December 2014. Bensouda again accused Kenya of blocking her work, but questions were also raised about the apparent weaknesses and lack of preparation in the prosecution case, which had largely been put together by Luis Moreno-Ocampo.[36] When the news broke, Kenyatta and Ruto were greeted by crowds of jubilant supporters, and a clearly gleeful Kenyatta took to Twitter to lambast the court's 'glaring lack of impartiality',[37] and called it the 'Toy of declining imperial powers'. In April 2016 the inevitable happened and the case against Ruto and Sang was thrown out by the court, with judges again decrying 'troubling incidence of witness interference and intolerable political interference' which had caused the case to collapse.[38] Although Ruto was not acquitted of the charges, the failure of the case was an astonishing blow to the ICC and a stunning victory for the African backlash against it. Many talked of the ICC having been 'discredited' by the case. Yet again thousands of victims of atrocities were left side-lined with seemingly little hope of justice.

The ICC has managed to a certain extent to stumble on from these difficulties. In 2014, the transitional government of CAR led by Catherine Samba Panza referred itself to the ICC for investigation. The court opened a new case looking into all human rights abuses perpetrated in the country since 2003, in particular the inter-ethnic violence which had erupted in the country from 2012 onwards, after former president François Bozizé was toppled by a rebel alliance. Thousands were killed and at one point a fifth of the population was displaced after Christian defence militias clashed with the mostly Muslim rebels across the country. This investigation into the roles of a small number of high-ranking individuals is still ongoing alongside a more general Special Court which is being created in CAR itself. In early 2016 Côte d'Ivoire's former president Laurent Gbagbo went on trial at the ICC in The Hague alongside his ally Charles Blé Goudé, accused of crimes against humanity in the violent aftermath of a disputed presidential election in 2010 which left around 3000 people dead. The ICC prosecutor alleged that Gbagbo attempted to stay in power by using the state's defence and security forces and political militias to target the supporters of his rival Alassane Ouattara, now Côte d'Ivoire's president. While this case has been welcomed by some quarters as a clear signal that former heads of state cannot expect to escape prosecution once out of power, the process has also been criticised for not pursuing claims of political violence committed by the winning side, giving rise to critiques of victor's justice.[39] Gbagbo's wife Simone, also wanted by the court, has yet to be handed over by the Ivorian authorities and was acquitted by a court in Abidjan in 2017.

In September 2016 the ICC scored a significant victory with the conviction of Ahmad al Faqi Al Mahdi as a co-perpetrator of the war crime consisting of intentionally directing attacks against religious and historic buildings.[40] Al Mahdi, who had been a member of the Ansar Dine jihadist group during the takeover of northern Mali by Islamist rebels in 2012, pleaded guilty to his role in destroying a number of ancient Sufi shrines and tombs in the historic city of Timbuktu, which his group had considered idolatrous. His conviction was historic in that it was the first time the destruction of cultural heritage had been prosecuted by the court, the first time the body had tried an Islamic radical, and the first time anyone had pleaded guilty (he had been recorded on camera smashing up the tombs and the footage had been shared widely on the internet, making a denial difficult). However, the case nevertheless managed to stir criticism, with some observers such as legal analyst Mark Kersten arguing that 'he was likely targeted by the ICC in part because he promised to co-operate with prosecutors',[41] and pointing out that the ICC had been unable to pursue charges of sexual violence in Mali.

African objections to the ICC ⟶ ▸ *Fatou Bedasu(?) quote*

It is important to stress that the picture across the African continent is not uniform. The ICC continues to enjoy wide support from a number of African countries, including Côte d'Ivoire, Nigeria, Mali, Ghana and DRC, which all vocally defended the institution at its annual meeting in late 2016. Nigeria, Senegal and others spoke out against the AU 'Withdrawal Strategy from the ICC' announced at the AU summit in Addis Ababa in July 2017.[42] Organisations such as HRW continue to support its work on behalf of a number of African civil society organisations, which see the court as one of the most powerful tools offering hope to ordinary African victims of human rights abuses. 'Some African leaders have beaten civil society in getting their message across', says William Nyarko, from the Africa Centre for International Law in Ghana. 'When we actually engage the public and help them to understand the court in a non-abstract way we find they are largely supportive.'[43]

Nevertheless, it is important to analyse the political objections to the ICC in order to understand what might prove useful or attractive from the experience of the EAC hybrid tribunal model. The African objections to the ICC fall into three broad categories: the perceived 'anti-African' bias, the threat to the principle of sitting head of state immunity and the danger that arrest warrants and prosecutions launched before fighting has ended may interrupt peace-making.

Much of the AU criticism, and in particular that voiced by figures such as Omar Al-Bashir and Uhuru Kenyatta, relates to the fact that all its investigations bar one – that into the Russia/Georgia war in South Ossetia in 2008 which was announced in January 2016 – have been in Africa. All thirty-nine people to have appeared in the dock in The Hague so far have been Africans,[44] although a number of preliminary examinations are ongoing in other areas, including that of Russian officials in Ukraine. Significantly in November 2017 the chief prosecutor requested permission to investigate US military personnel and members of the CIA over allegations of war crimes in Afghanistan, as well as members of the Afghan security forces, the Taliban and the Haqqani network.

This focus on African crimes had led to accusations of neo-colonialism. While it is vital not to forget that several of these cases – Uganda, DRC, Côte d'Ivoire, CAR and Mali for example – were all self-referrals by African leaders, when voiced by the likes of Ruto and Kenyatta during their political battles with the ICC these accusations of bias proved particularly pernicious. The ICC also seems to have offended some African nations by its interpretation of the 'complementarity' principle – specifically that it has been perceived at times to have stepped in too quickly, overriding ongoing national processes and leaving a sense that they were deemed to be inadequate. For example, in the DRC there were already domestic trials ongoing against all four of the Ituri warlords indicted by the ICC, but these trials were not completed before the four men were hurriedly transferred to The Hague (albeit with the seeming cooperation of the government). Steps like these have been seized upon as evidence of African leaders and justice systems being undermined.

To defuse the criticism the argument has been made that the ICC cannot be biased, or even racist, because it has African officials, including crucially the new chief prosecutor, Fatou Bensouda, who replaced Luis Moreno-Ocampo in 2012. However, this has also been dismissed by a number of analysts, including Tor Krever, who claims 'to identify African officials in the court's leadership is a red herring ... Insisting that Bensouda doesn't have a biased agenda is very different from suggesting that the court ... [is] subject to political pressures'.[45] This impression of bias has been bolstered over the years as the US appeared to escape justice over the Iraq War, and then indeed began to influence the court's work by courting domestic public opinion in order to see villains such as Joseph Kony apprehended and the 'genocidal' Darfur conflict resolved. At the same time, there has been little progress in attempting to indict Bashir Al-Assad in Syria (although Syria is not a signatory), Russian officials over Ukraine (again not a signatory), while Luis Moreno-Ocampo jumped headlong into an investigation into crimes committed by the Libyan authorities under Colonel Qaddafi in the aftermath of the Arab Spring – an investigation which some claimed went hand-in-hand with the NATO-led bombardment of Libya. The fact that cases have been referred by the UN Security Council – three of whose members are not even members of the court themselves – has also provoked charges of a neo-colonialist attitude. 'No honest, self-reflecting advocate of international criminal justice can say he or she is satisfied with the reach of the ICC', argues Mark Kesten. 'It *is* selective and that *is* a problem.'[46]

The threat to the principle of sitting heads of state immunity – a central tenet of the AU – has also helped stoke the flames of resentment. The indictments against Uhuru Kenyatta and Omar Al-Bashir proved deeply unpopular in some quarters, and appear to have been a major factor in propelling South Africa to announce its withdrawal, particularly with the country's much criticised refusal to arrest Al Bashir when he visited Pretoria in 2015.[47] In 2009 the AU decided that its members had no legal responsibility to arrest the Sudanese president, a fact which no doubt encouraged his continent-wide travel and gave governments the confidence to let him leave their territory a free man. While the Rome Statute was drafted to reflect the idea that the international community has a responsibility to see that international crimes are punished, 'African leaders appear unable to accept the inroads made into the immunity of sitting heads of state by the Al Bashir warrant', argues Rowland J.V. Cole.[48]

Another serious concern has been the effect that the threat of judicial proceedings against one party in an ongoing conflict has had on the chances of securing peace. This was clearly demonstrated by Joseph Kony's insistence on the dropping of the arrest warrants before he would agree to enter peace talks with Ugandan government negotiators. As Phil Clark explains, 'The Kony case was a watershed. Once an ICC arrest warrant is issued it's almost impossible to get rid of it'.[49] The debate about the relative merits of criminal prosecutions versus other approaches including amnesties and reintegration of former fighters in resolving conflicts is still far from settled, as the recent difficulties of passing the referendum on a peace deal which granted amnesty to some members of the rebel FARC (Revolutionary Armed Forces of Colombia) movement in Colombia showed. In 2008 the AU Peace and Security Council declared that the arrest warrant issued against Omar Al-Bashir was a threat to the ongoing Darfur peace negotiations, although up until that point the AU peace process had had little notable impact. As the case of the expelled aid workers in Darfur demonstrates, the arrest warrants even threatened to reignite the conflict and make things worse for those who had survived atrocities before a comprehensive peace had been established. 'With the arrest warrants hanging over him, might Bashir feel the time was right to go on an all-out offensive to find a military solution in Africa?', asked journalist Rob Crilly.[50] Again when Kenyatta and Ruto were summoned to The Hague, the proceedings were viewed by the AU as a hindrance to efforts to negotiate a coalition government.

Rob Crilly's analysis of the Darfur conflict and the calls from US-based groups such as the Save Darfur coalition for prosecutions of African despots even as the fighting still rages, clearly highlights 'black and white' attitudes to right and wrong and the imperative for justice.[51] He argues that these oversimplifications can risk interrupting complex and delicate locally sensitive solutions to conflict. Tim Allen, writing about Uganda, has referred to the 'dangers of "international law fundamentalism"',[52] where the need to prosecute in recent years appears to have overridden traditional community reconciliation processes and alternatives sources of justice. Even processes such as South Africa's 1994 Truth and Reconciliation Commission, which focused on victims and witnesses talking about their experiences as a form of restorative justice, and the Gacaca 'community' courts following the Rwandan genocide, which were designed to promote reconciliation, have been questioned and seen as 'illegitimate' by some.

In addition, there appears to have been a notable 'cooling off' of the ICC's initial enthusiasm for promoting the role of victims in trials, something on which the court initially hoped to focus. As Phil Clark explained, the participation of victims was seen to be becoming unwieldy. Despite early lofty promises of 'Trust Funds', the ICC has a poor reputation when it comes to securing reparations for victims. For example, DRC warlord Thomas Lubanga was convicted in 2012, but at the time of writing the court had still not even formally identified the full list of victims who qualified for compensation.

Despite the promising start, in just fifteen years the ICC has gone from appearing to offer hope to many African countries struggling with violence and human rights abuses to appearing to be on an outright collision course with some countries on the continent. In October 2016, Burundi, the Gambia and South Africa all announced their intention to pull out of the ICC. The Burundian decision appeared to be linked the opening of a UN investigation into alleged human rights abuses committed during a protest movement against Pierre Nkurunziza's attempt to stand for a third term as president. The Gambia's decision, which was a personal blow to Chief Prosecutor Fatou Bensouda, who is Gambian, in all but words accused the court of being racist.[53] Gambia said it was unhappy that the ICC had refused to investigate the deaths of thousands of migrants from sub-Saharan Africa trying to cross the Mediterranean Sea to reach Europe. However, the decision to pull out was reversed in 2017 by Adama Barrow, the country's new president, who beat Yahya Jammeh in elections in late 2016. South Africa's decision – also subsequently the subject of a legal and constitutional challenge – was lamented because of South Africa's leading position on human rights and justice in the post-apartheid era and the fact that South Africa had been one of the court's biggest early supporters. These three countries are not alone; Uganda, Namibia and Chad have expressed an interest in withdrawing, as has Kenya, undoubtedly scarred by its own experience with the institution. And the idea of leaving the ICC appears to be on the agenda at the highest levels of African politics. At the AU summit in January 2017, an 'ICC Withdrawal Strategy' was announced by a number of states. The document made specific reference to the controversial head of state immunity issue, although it appeared to be non-binding,[54] without concrete steps or a timeline.

Evaluation of the EAC regionalised hybrid model

The EAC was an ad hoc hybrid trial conceived at a time when much academic literature had assumed that hybrids would cease to be relevant as the ICC assumed its full powers. In fact, as Phil Clark puts it, 'Hybrids have lived on and we're now seeing a real mish-mash of models'.[55] It has become obvious that there are many situations the ICC will not be able to investigate and prosecute, and the success of the EAC is further proof that there is still a role for hybrid trials.

In addition, there are particular features of the EAC which made it popular in Africa, and these must also be considered in future attempts to set up prosecutions. From the outset the EAC seemed immune from that most serious charge of being institutionally biased or even racist: it was a court set up by Africans and could therefore hardly be criticised for targeting Africans. While some criticised the 'limited' internationalisation of the EAC, which in effect boiled down to just two judges from outside Senegal, they were nevertheless African officials, not Europeans. This was a symbolic, political victory, a court which could defend itself against charges of being imperialist. While it secured the approval of the Chadian authorities – which didn't challenge its legitimacy and in fact provided 35% of its budget – it was also the first time the AU itself had been involved in setting up an internationalised criminal tribunal. All the judges and prosecution team were Africans, and the only white faces were a handful of European lawyers who assisted in the civil parties' representation. It was a politically acceptable formula and has shown that the AU has the capacity to try the most serious international crimes.

Nevertheless, some of the EAC's failings show that, like all courts, including the ICC, it still came up against political realities which compromised its work. For example, it was unable to secure the extradition of the five co-accused and many have suggested that was because of political blockages at the highest levels in Chadian politics. This is an interesting point, as the ICC has so far only succeeding in jailing a number of relatively low-ranking individuals such as Lubanga and Bemba, both rebel leaders who were operating somewhat on the side-lines of bigger geo-political conflicts. Its attempts to go after the leaders of Sudan and Kenya have failed. The EAC by contrast got the top man, which is no mean achievement, but failed to get the middle-ranking people who may well have been responsible for the day-to-day human rights abuses and actually may have had more answers than Habré himself. This leaves the question of whether a court should go for the high-profile politically difficult cases, risking an immediate backlash if they fail, or whether its prosecutors should aim for the cases they know they can win. It might seem that whichever it chooses, a court cannot really win.

Delayed justice

The EAC's success in pursuing abuses by a leader who had presumably assumed he would never have to answer for his actions thirty years before is an interesting test case, and opens up questions about whether such a hybrid trial model could be useful in pursuing cases of historical abuses. The general direction of some of the debate since the ICTY and ICTR has been that serious international crimes need to be prosecuted more quickly – that justice delayed is justice denied, as in the case of Slobodan Milosevic, who died before his trial was concluded. As we have seen, the ICC's permanent status has been viewed as a plus as it has enabled it to begin investigations before civil conflicts have been concluded. However, as Alex Whiting, professor at Harvard Law school, has argued, not every delay in the case of war crimes is necessarily a bad thing: 'As states, non-state groups and individuals move beyond the conflict, they may be more inclined to provide information and evidence for war crimes investigations, either because they in time recognise that it is in their self-interest to do so, or because passions have sufficiently cooled to make co-operation possible'.[56]

With regard to the AU's objection to the idea of prosecuting *sitting* heads of state, the success of the EAC suggests that there may in time be more political will at the regional level to go after leaders once they have left power. Sometimes this may take decades, but political trials can be held only when the political conditions are right, a point which also links to the criticisms that ICC arrest warrants have in some cases appeared to interfere in both ongoing high-level diplomatic peace initiatives and community efforts to bring reconciliation.

Of course, the threat of a retroactive prosecution needs to be balanced against the danger of appearing to do nothing as crimes are being committed. It also creates a precarious situation where a sitting head of state may feel that without the trappings of power and head of state immunity, they may one day have to answer for their crimes. This was dramatically demonstrated in late 2016, when Gambia's president Yahya Jammeh abruptly decided to cling onto power, after initially promising to respect the results of an election which had been won by his rival Adama Barrow. There were suggestions that a threat to prosecute Jammeh over human rights abuses and the stealing of state assets by Barrow's supporters was a key factor in his attempt to hang onto power.[57] Although Jammeh was eventually persuaded to step down by his fellow West African statesmen and an an arguably expedient decision was made to withdraw the threat of prosecution, it may not be a coincidence that he chose to go into exile in Equatorial Guinea, which does not recognise the ICC.

Can it be repeated?

The EAC has offered the prospect of trying historical cases of human rights abuses, using a politically legitimate 'all-African' hybrid trial model. But before we jump to the conclusion that the EAC Statute should just be dusted off and used again (for example in a prosecution of Jammeh), it is important to remember that the EAC as an institution was a very particular response to a very particular set of circumstances. Hissène Habré was an exceptionally isolated figure by the time the trial finally opened, some twenty-five years after he had been ousted. He was in exile, abandoned by his former supporters such as the US and France, and for most of the 2000s his only powerful protector was Abdoulaye Wade. Many of his fellow contemporary African despots had died or been forced from power. When Macky Sall assumed office in 2012, changing the political conditions at the highest level in Senegal, and without doubt 'the most significant development which changed the course of our campaign', according to Reed Brody,[58] his protection evaporated and it was relatively easy politically to hand him over. Twenty years after he left power, and the complexities of rebel groups in Chad having moved on significantly from Habré loyalists, there was little danger of anyone objecting to the EAC arrest warrants due to their potential derailing of domestic peace negotiations. In the early stages of the investigation, Chad seemed keen to assist and facilitate the trial's progress and Habré no longer had enough popular support in Chad to save him. However, as we have seen, fears soon began to emerge that the EAC's focus on other DDS agents still at liberty in Chad was making key figures in today's administration uncomfortable.

In terms of setting up a replica ad hoc hybrid trial to try a former head of state for historical human rights abuses, it is therefore hard to think of many other such 'dictators waiting in the wings' who have been out of power a long time and would be so vulnerable to prosecution. One possibility might be Ethiopia's former dictator Haile Mariam Mengistu, who lived for many years in Harare under the protection of Robert Mugabe, although it's so far unclear what impact the fall of Mugabe will have on the former leader's position in Zimbabwe. Just as the research for this book was being completed, serious effort was being put into the idea of prosecuting Gambia's former leader Yahya Jammeh, and investigating human rights abuses and the stealing of state assets during his twenty-two-year rule. Reed Brody has signalled his interest in helping the Gambian victims with this case,[59] and a number of Habré's victims travelled to the Gambia in early 2017 to talk to survivors of abuse there about their experience of mounting a prosecution.[60] Nevertheless, a prima facie look at the situation suggests that it might be difficult to ensure a prosecution of Jammeh without the cooperation of the Equatorial Guinean authorities.

The road that led to the design of the EAC was long, tortuous and very specific. It involved failed bids to prosecute Habré using Senegal's domestic courts, Belgium's (now rescinded) universal jurisdiction law and finally a questionable ruling by the ECOWAS court that led to 'internationalisation' of a trial which could possibly in other circumstances have been held in domestic courts. The ICC was unable to prosecute because the crimes were committed before 1998. In addition, despite Idriss Déby Itno being Habré's nemesis, Chad effectively gave up its right to charge and try Habré in a domestic court, possibly because of fears that too much information would come out about former DDS agents and Habré-era associates. Any future attempts at prosecution will see all alternative routes – ICC and domestic – explored, and might not necessarily conclude that setting up a new court from scratch is the best approach.

It is also important to consider to what extent the support of well-funded international organisations such as HRW and Amnesty International enabled the case to reach a conclusion. Reed Brody's life was taken over for sixteen years, as he himself confesses, because his friendships with people such as Jacqueline Moudeina and Clement Abaifouta gave him a sense of purpose. Although the Chadian victims and figures such as Moudeina, Abaifouta and Souleymane Guengueng have gone to incredible lengths to present their case around the world, it is hard to imagine they would have been able to reach the global audience they did without the help of HRW – a large, well-known US organisation with a global communications team. HRW has numerous experienced and qualified lawyers who were lucky enough to have time and money to think of alternatives approaches as the Belgium, Chad and Senegal prosecutions floundered. Reed Brody was sufficiently well-known to be able to generate significant fund-raising from international institutions and influential individuals to help pay for his own position and for a team of researchers to help him prepare for the case – a figure thought to have reached at least $1.5 million over sixteen years.[61]

Universal jurisdiction

Another key consideration in repeating the EAC model is to understand to what extent the concept of universal jurisdiction might play in any future tribunal. Universal jurisdiction was a major 'unique' pillar of the EAC, because previous tribunals have relied primarily on the exercise of territorial jurisdiction. As academic Sarah Williams argues, 'The EAC now sets a precedent for the creation of an internationalised criminal tribunal that operates exclusively on the basis of universal jurisdiction'.[62] In theory, universal jurisdiction could be very attractive because it removes the difficulty of finding a multi-country consensus for any kind of trial to take place, and has in fact been promoted as a useful tool by groups such as African Legal Aid.[63]

Nevertheless, just as the US had feared the creation of a chief prosecutor at the ICC with powers to indict sitting heads of state around the world, the AU has also recently become suspicious of the potential abuse of universal jurisdiction. It has become associated with attempts by European judges to override judicial processes elsewhere – for example the Pinochet case, and significantly for the AU the decision in 2008 by a Spanish judge to issue international arrests warrants using universal jurisdiction against forty Rwandan officials, accusing them of revenge killings following the 1994 genocide, and crimes against humanity, genocide and terrorism.[64] One of these figures, Karenzi Karake, the head of Rwanda's intelligence services, was arrested at Heathrow Airport in July 2015, although the extradition request was turned down. This universal jurisdiction case caused a furious backlash from Rwanda's president Paul Kagame, who took the issue to the AU's Peace and Security Council. The body responded with a stinging rebuke that criticised Western governments for 'a blatant violation of the principle of universal jurisdiction ... Not only an attack on a Rwandan national, but on Africa as a whole'.[65] In other words, universal jurisdiction can be seen as a rogue action by one state, undermining the international order: 'it may well be that states would consider that trials based on universal jurisdiction are in fact more offensive to and dangerous for dominant concepts of sovereignty than trials which at least have the legitimacy and imprimatur of the international community'.[66]

Part of the AU's motivation to create the EAC was because of the threat to extradite the former African head of state to Belgium, which was exercising its own universal jurisdiction, seen by some as a 'neo-colonialist move'. This is somewhat perplexing as the EAC case eventually came to rest on Senegal's right to exercise universal jurisdiction. Sarah Williams has argued that the eventual decision to use universal jurisdiction at the EAC does not necessarily undermine the AU's position because the body was able to carefully influence and shape the establishment of the court, and because it was an African country exercising universal jurisdiction.[67] However it remains to be seen if any potential future trials, particularly anything conceived by the AU, would want specifically to open the door to future reliance on this legal concept.

In conclusion, the EAC's real value was that it secured a conviction in a reasonably short time and without drama. While the ICC was accused of an anti-African bias, the EAC was a court created by the AU itself. It had legitimacy because it allowed international (but crucially African) participation, saving it from the worst charge of neo-colonialism. There was also little to stoke the political objections at the leadership level in Africa. Its focus on historical abuses and the decision not to investigate Idriss Déby side-stepped the issue of head of state immunity, and its retroactive mandate meant that sufficient time had passed in Chad to allow passions to cool, meaning it had limited impact on contemporary Chadian politics. Habré can be seen as a politically acceptable sacrifice, helping the AU to show that it is willing and able to tackle impunity for the most serious of crimes, including torture, crimes against humanity and war crimes.

As the one-size-fits-all 'permanent court' model of the ICC based in Europe continues to be challenged across Africa, the winding road to the establishment of the EAC is an interesting lesson in pragmatic, flexible and innovative solutions to political deadlocks. It has challenged the idea that authoritarian leaders can reasonably expect to retire into obscurity and never have to answer for their crimes. Furthermore, it has shown that ordinary people can get together, stand up and take on former leaders who were once able to terrorise them. Although it is questionable that we will see an exact replica of the court mechanism due to the unpopularity of the universal jurisdiction principle, the success of the EAC has shown that ad hoc hybrid courts set up by the AU can play an important role in future efforts to seek justice on the African continent.

CONCLUSION

Lessons Learned

With no further appeals allowed under the EAC, the temporary chamber has been dissolved and this verdict brings to an end an extraordinary saga in African politics and historical justice. Hissène Habré, once inspiring awe and fear in equal measure, the 'little God' who ruled over Chad with an iron fist for eight years, has been unmasked as a simple human being, unable to call on his former supporters the US and France to save him from spending the rest of his life in prison. The cruel and brutal methods he sanctioned in order to cling onto power have been revealed to the world, along with the shocking methods employed by his network of secret police and torturers which enforced his power. The idea that former leaders can expect to escape judgement for their crimes has been challenged: 'We've shone a light on impunity', says Jacqueline Moudeina. 'That's what this was really all about.'[1] This remarkable achievement has been brought about by the tireless dedication of a small number of Chadian lawyers and victims who refused ever to give up. As Reed Brody has acknowledged in his many post-trial analyses, the voices of victims have been central to this process, and enormous credit must be given to these campaigners who brought a dictator to justice.

At the same time, the EAC set up within the Senegalese court system proved to a large extent to be competent and professional, avoiding so many of the pitfalls which have dogged African justice in the past. The court kept meticulously on schedule and budget and was not derailed by Habré's histrionic refusal to cooperate at the _eginning. The EAC has been widely welcomed as an example of the AU showing its commitment to trying those accused of human rights abuses in the past, in many ways being viewed as an 'African solution to an African problem'. Through its location on African soil, the use of African administrators and judges and the strong participation of Chadian lawyers and victims registered as civil parties, it has offered an interesting alternative to the idea of a biased and even 'racist' ICC handing out justice from distant European courtrooms. There has also been a knock-on impact on Senegalese justice, which has commendably shown its capability to try international crimes, with a number of key figures such as Mbacké Fall now able to boast impressive experience in handling international cases.

The EAC also made impressive but less well-publicised strides in developing the concept of outreach and community and engagement with its work. There was a sustained campaign of sensitisation in Chad itself, as well as the much-welcomed four *commissions rogatoires* led by Chief Prosecutor Mbacké Fall, which appear to have gone a long way to convincing victims and ordinary Chadians alike that the court was there to listen to them and that the justice it would deliver would be theirs. From my interviews with victims in Chad and through covering the case, I believe that many of them are satisfied with the verdict and sentence; of the people that I interviewed in N'Djamena (of course this was not an exhaustive list), most expressed relief that a twenty-five-year campaign for justice, with its seemingly never-ending blind alleys of failed prosecutions and delays, has ended with a significant outcome. These victims talked about how the verdict had changed their life and allowed them to move on from the horrors of the past. As my survey revealed, there was also relief and joy over the verdict among ordinary Chadians: 'Not only are the victims proud, but all Chadians and Africans', claimed Christian Mbaidoum; 'This is a historic verdict. It's the first time an African president has been judged on African soil', reflected Alladoum Le-Ngarhoulem; 'This is proof that we can judge heads of state who thought they could kill their own people.

It shows that Africa can have its own international criminal court', said Leopold Dinanou.[2]

Nevertheless, the EAC has not succeeded at everything. Facing budget and duration pressures, it was forced from the beginning to limit the scope of its investigations. While it can be commended for realising the importance of indicting Habré's five trusted lieutenants in order to fully understand the complexity of the DDS command structures in the 1980s, it was ultimately unable to bring the co-accused to trial. Frustratingly for many who had hoped that the trial would be able to shed more light on who actually gave the orders, Habré was reduced to a silent and vague presence wrapped in white robes always on the periphery of an electrifying court process. We will probably never know the full extent of what really happened in Chad from 1982 to 1990 and exactly how much of it was personally ordered by Habré. The EAC was not able to establish a reliable figure for the number of people who are believed to have died from abuse, maltreatment and as part of organised massacres in Chad under Habré's rule. While the court-appointed defence team did their best in almost impossible circumstances, the inadequacy of the defence was clear to see. The court also chose to avoid examining the role of international support from the US and France in perpetuating the brutalities of the DDS torture. 'I had mixed feelings when the verdict came in', said Amnesty International Chad researcher Gaetan Mootoo, who worked on Chad throughout the 1980s.

> Although I was happy to see an end to it, I remembered all those who died before they got justice because it had all taken so long. I saw representatives from the international community in the court that day, and wondered if they did not feel hypocritical. What were they all doing in the 1980s when Chadian victims were crying out for help?[3]

The EAC has also proved incapable of launching a serious investigation into recovering the money that Habré allegedly stole from Chad during the 1980s and from the country's treasury on the night he was toppled by Idriss Déby. So far only around $900,000 has been recovered, a fraction of that promised to victims in reparations. Funding constraints and gaps in the statute have left major questions regarding who is ultimately responsible for ensuring that the victims receive the compensation they have been promised, and this has not been comprehensively solved with the dissolution of the Appeals Chamber. The Trust Fund has yet to be established, and a donor's conference to accept pledges for the Fund has been repeatedly postponed. At the same time there appears to be no discernible impact on the Chadian justice system, although the handful of Chadian lawyers who stood before the bar may be able to use their hands-on experience in international law in the future. Although many observers believe that the case provided enough of a scare for current President Idriss Déby Itno to at least initially promise to cooperate, there has been no significant improvement in Chadian democracy over the last few years. Although some major figures from the DDS are now behind bars in Chad, there are still a number of former agents at large in the country, and some of his former supporters are still in positions of power. These points show that the EAC, like any other international criminal justice process, will always come up against political blockages to its work.

Nevertheless, in the end it may well be that a seemingly incomplete justice is viewed as better than no justice at all. For the victims the issue of outstanding compensation is a bitter pill to swallow, but there remains a strong sense of satisfaction that at least Habré is behind bars and that their suffering has been widely recognised. The EAC aimed extremely high and succeeded in jailing the actual commander in chief. This is no mean accomplishment. In terms of the failure to examine the role of the US and France in supporting Habré, as far as international criminal cases go, some observers believe that it is not unusual that the political and historical circumstances surrounding the committing of human rights abuses are not examined. 'The question of international involvement always comes up', says Emmanuelle Marchand, who helped Alain Werner prepare for the trial and who has worked on a number of international cases. 'People asked at the ECCC about the impact of US bombing in Cambodia. But international justice is always narrow – can we be expected to deal with everything?'[4] It seems that it often proves impractical for reasons of time and money to go into detail about every facet of the political system surrounding human rights abuses, and seems likely that legal professionals will choose the cases that they believe they are most likely to win. Choices will always have to be made about the number of people to try and their relative seniority. *not tried if too senior? Isn't that whole point?!*

The AU view

The EAC was an ad hoc 'hybrid' or internationalised trial which was conceived at a time when much academic literature had assumed the days of hybrid courts were over and the ICC would become a natural 'next step' for justice. It was, significantly, the first time the courts of one African country had been used to prosecute crimes in another African country using the principle of universal jurisdiction. It therefore offered an alternative model to the assumed primacy of the ICC and could 'provide valuable insight into what a regional approach to internationalised justice may look like'.[5] Specifically for the EAC, that included the welcome prospect of no Europeans on the prosecution team or the judge's bench, as well as Chadian lawyers defending Chadian victims on Senegalese soil. This appears to have given the court legitimacy because no longer could charges of international justice being dictated from distant courtrooms in Europe hold much water, and the EAC prosecution of Habré has been hailed as 'a valuable learning experience' for all concerned.[6] The case was constructed on a very specific basis and the international elements have helped bolster the foundation of the Senegalese justice system, increasing its legitimacy, and has also shown that the AU is able to to deal with situations of impunity.

Much now depends on what the AU decides to do with its experience of setting up the EAC. As the only pan-African body with the expertise and legislative power to set up these kinds of trials, it seems that the issue of political will at the level of the AU leadership is key to taking forward the experience of Habré's prosecution.

The AU could of course do nothing, as the Dakar trial was only ever meant to be a prosecution of Hissène Habré. However, the regional grouping initially seemed proud of the court and keen to showcase its role in developing 'African solutions to African problems'. Reed Brody has said that the role of individuals such as the AU's former legal counsel Ben Kioko in setting up the EAC in negotiations with Senegal in 2013 was crucial. At the AU summit in Johannesburg in 2015, which took place as the EAC opened its doors for the first time in Senegal, the AU's new legal counsel Vincent Nmehielle said that it was 'an example of the AU managing its own judicial affairs as it was best placed to do so as it best understood them'.[7] However, as the EAC proceedings developed, there was a sense in some quarters that the AU voice was becoming less prominent in the debate. Some openly questioned whether the body's support for the institution had cooled, and whether a common position on the commitment to try future cases of human rights abuses existed. There was no permanent representative based in Dakar to cover the case,[8] and AU comments were often lacking in the news reports.

However, just days after the verdict, a meeting was organised in Dakar which brought together a number of prominent figures in international criminal justice to discuss the verdict, including the AU's Vincent Nmehielle and Baltazar Garzon, the pioneering Spanish judge who was behind the universal jurisdiction arrest warrant issued against Augusto Pinochet. At this meeting, Nmehielle said that the EAC was 'a historic victory for the AU who has always had the intention to try Africans'.[9] The event was organised by African Legal Aid, which also organised a meeting in The Hague to discuss the Habré legacy, and a seminar on 'Carrying

Forward the Legacy of the Extraordinary African Chambers in the Trial of Hissène Habré' as a side event at the AU summit in Addis Ababa in July 2017. This seminar was well-attended, even being addressed by the Chadian AU Commission chairperson and the Ministers of Justice of Senegal and Chad. According to Evelyn Ankumah, director of African Legal Aid, the biggest success of the trial appeared to be symbolic, with many of the participants welcoming its 'legitimacy', 'Even if some African heads of state do not relish the prospect of one day being held to account if they were to leave power after committing abuses, no one could accuse the EAC of being imperialists'.[10] Despite these warm declarations of support, there were few concrete proposals put forward at the event about how the success of the trial could practically be built upon.

There may be a number of explanations for some of this ambivalence. For a start there was the ongoing background of high-level AU disputes with the ICC over the issue of head of state immunity and the lack of a common position on that and other questions of justice between African leaders. Although there appeared to be broad agreement when Macky Sall was elected that it was indeed time to bring an end to the Habré story, there has nevertheless been a sense that the Senegalese leader's decision has not played well with everyone. On the day of the verdict, there was a sense of backtracking. The Senegalese Justice Minister said that Habré could be in line for a 'pardon', and there were a number of rumours that Habré's sentence could be commuted to a lesser term or that he might be allowed to gracefully retire to a friendly country such as Morocco to finish his sentence under house arrest. As the case of Yahya Jammeh so clearly demonstrates, there is a very real danger of dictators trying to hang onto power if the threat of prosecution looms over them after they have lost the trappings of head of state immunity. At the same time, Chad's influence has been growing at the heart of the AU. As we have seen, there was some speculation that the EAC's increasing reach was creating discomfort in Chad. With Idriss Déby elected as chair of the AU in 2016, and his former Foreign Minister Moussa Faki Mahamat elected as the chair of the AU commission in 2017, the issue of investigating historical abuses by former leaders may well find itself dropping off the agenda.

What can be repeated

It is essential to ask what aspects can practically be carried forward and what a future trial might look like. One possible approach is the idea of creating a team of 'roving' African judges experienced in trying international crimes, supported by a basic template statute similar to that of the EAC which could be grafted onto local laws to create similar ad hoc hybrid bodies to respond to specific situations. This list of experienced personnel could now reasonably include the Burkinabe Gustave Gberdao Kam and the Malian Wafi Ouaga-deye, who presided over the Trial and Appeals Chambers of the EAC. This approach, of course, would need political will from the countries concerned, but could provide a quick, mobile response to human rights abuses: 'innovative building and borrowing', as Phil Clark puts it.[11]

In fact, we are already witnessing a number of similar attempts to set up African ad hoc trials, and the feasibility of the 'roving' model approach has recently been given a huge boost by the news in February 2017 that the president of CAR, Faustin Touadera, has appointed a Congolese judge Toussaint Muntazini Mukimapa as special prosecutor of a new Special Criminal Court set up by the CAR's transitional government in 2015. Muntazini finally arrived in Bangui in May 2017. The Special Court has the support of the UN peacekeeping mission in CAR and was created following thousands of inter-ethnic and religious killings and mass displace-ments which followed the toppling of François Bozizé by the Seleka rebel alliance in 2013.[12] It also has power to investigate all violence and human rights abuses carried out in the country since 2003. Crucially, it is envisaged that this court will be a kind of hybrid, including a mix of international and domestic staff and laws but based entirely within the CAR domestic system. Perhaps in this case, the statute of the EAC could be of use to those establishing the court and lessons can be learned from the value of an 'all-African' experience and how that relates to the domestic system. It is also significant that the new CAR court will operate alongside parallel investigations by the ICC in CAR which are looking into the role of more high-level suspects, showing there is still willingness from some African states for the ICC to work in tandem with domestic or hybrid justice systems. Nevertheless, the court will face huge challenges, including accessing witnesses in areas where civil conflict is ongoing and being clear about overlapping jurisdiction with the ICC, and it will undoubtedly have to be selective about which cases it pursues.[13] At the same time, it is questionable to what extent this would be an African court as so far it is unclear if its funding will come from the AU.

In South Sudan too, an ad hoc hybrid court was proposed as a key aspect of a 2015 peace deal aimed at bringing an end to the devastating civil conflict between the rival supporters of President Salva Kiir and his former vice president Riek Machar, which broke out in 2013. In principle this court (the Hybrid Court for South Sudan, HCSS) was to have the power to prosecute war crimes, crimes against humanity and genocide, and was to include a number of South Sudanese judges working alongside African counterparts. However, in this case political will seems to be lacking and crucially there still appears to be no end in sight to the fighting. The establishment of the court has been repeatedly delayed, partly due to apparent resistance from both Kiir and Machar, who may both fear being hauled before the court themselves. As South Sudan is not a signatory to the ICC, this takes us back to the thorny issue of sitting heads of state. Kiir has hinted at a preference for a 'national dialogue', for the hybrid court to be based in a third country, and to be on an equal footing with parallel domestic judicial processes. These all suggest that South Sudanese authorities could seek to derail the court's investigative work and independence.[14] In this case, the experience of the Habré trial could be invaluable in helping the AU search for possible independent third-party venues and to establish exactly how much (or little) 'internationalisation' is politically acceptable.

Another possible avenue would be to create a permanent hybrid body based in an African country that would contain a mix of domestic and African legal personnel and legislation, a 'regionalised' hybrid that could be as simple as just two judges not from the country which hosts it. Given its experience setting up the EAC within its court system, Senegal could feasibly be an obvious host for such a court. Senegal has now passed the necessary legislation giving it the jurisdiction to try international crimes, including universal jurisdiction powers to arrest anyone suspected of serious crimes on Senegalese territory. It is also now possible for anyone resident in Senegal, but not a Senegalese citizen, to bring a case in front of the Senegalese courts for human rights abuses carried out elsewhere. Chief prosecutor at the EAC, Mbacké Fall, certainly thinks this is a good way forward, arguing that Senegal can now prosecute cases which are difficult in domestic courts: 'We could start prosecuting individuals accused of international terrorism charges on behalf of other countries if the victims are able to meet our residency requirements'.[15]

It is questionable, though, if this idea will be able to take off as is it appears to mirror the current attempt by the AU to set up the new African Court of Justice and Human Rights. This would be a permanent court based in Arusha, Tanzania, and created by the merger of the African Court on Human and Peoples' Rights, established in 1998, and the Court of Justice of the African Union, established in 2003. This 'African court' has been viewed by some as the AU's response to the ICC. The court promises a number of interesting developments, including having jurisdiction to prosecute companies guilty of crimes committed in Africa as well as human trafficking and piracy. However, it has been criticised for granting immunity to heads of state and has so far made slow progress. Hot on the heels of his failed prosecution by the ICC, the Kenyan president Uhuru Kenyatta launched a bid at the AU summit in 2015 to try and fast-track the creation of the court, but his initiative fell flat when only eleven of fifty-four member states signed the proposed 'Malabo Protocol'.[16] Only nine countries have so far signed up for the new AU court,[17] short of the fifteen ratifications required. Even if there is not yet any clear political will to move this process forward, the AU has made noises that it is more interested in focusing its efforts on the Malabo Protocol, making it hard to imagine any energy for creating a second permanent hybrid.

What seems important to consider is the amount of political will that exists to deal with a particular problem at any given time. While the EAC demonstrated that the AU was capable of organising a cheap, quick and effective trial to prosecute the most serious human rights abuses on the continent, other proposed ad hoc hybrid bodies may never get off the ground. As we have seen, Habré was essentially an easy target, and with the election of Macky Sall in 2012 enough time had passed to make any possible trial politically desirable. The former president's protections in Senegal and Chad had melted away, Chad did not dispute the court's jurisdiction, Senegal was stung by the ICJ's judgment against it in 2012 and seemed to want to restore its reputation as a leader in justice, and the victims were aided by well-funded international lawyers willing and able to search for new methods of trying him. In other words, the creation of the EAC followed a unique and very difficult to repeat confluence of events, essentially a dogged campaign by activists ground into an impasse which was only broken by a seismic change at the top of Senegalese politics.

Nevertheless, aspects of the case will be carried forward, with perhaps the EAC's most symbolic victory simply being achieving a verdict. Although there are of course many other ways to approach dealing with cases of grave human rights abuses, the sections of the African judiciary and human rights community that believe in the importance of prosecutions must surely now be questioning whether it can be an alternative approach to the 'one size fits all' ICC. Discussions have already taken place in Senegal, at the AU summit, The Hague and Gambia about how the success of the EAC can be built upon. Early work is being put into the idea of prosecuting Yahya Jammeh, who looks as close to Habré's pariah status as can be imagined; in the absence of a strong court system in Gambia itself this could theoretically involve an ad hoc hybrid tribunal outside of the Gambia using the principle of universal jurisdiction. Whatever form these processes might take, the EAC's success as an African hybrid, together with its politically less sensitive historical viewpoint, look likely to be built upon.

The last word

Seemingly in reasonable health, Hissène Habré will most likely have a long time to contemplate his life, choices and fate. As he stares at the walls in Cap Manuel maison d'arrêt in Dakar, who knows if he looks back on his decision to remain silent during his trial with regret. What at first seemed like yet another egregious but potentially effective ambush on justice, a brazen attempt to discredit the EAC as 'imperialist', the histrionics on the first day of the case have faded into memory and all that remains is the image of his smouldering silence and growing impotence in front of the court. I still don't really understand why he chose to remain silent. I made a number of attempts to contact Habré through his supporter's website and his French lawyer François Serres, but I was unable to. The best insights I have as to his motivations for the non-cooperation are from two men who spent years hunting him down. Reed Brody says:

> Habré is an incredibly stubborn man. Within his framework he
> feels principled and I think he just didn't think he would get a
> fair trial. But you saw as the case went on, and perhaps as he got

more concerned that things were not going his way, he started to cooperate through his family talking outside court. But it would have been incredibly hard for a man of his self-esteem to ever accept that he was wrong.[18]

Chief Prosecutor Mbacké Fall says: 'He really just despised the court. He questioned our legitimacy. *C'est un homme du desert quoi* (He's a desert warrior)'.[19] Perhaps he will die with his secrets still intact.

The last word in this incredible story goes to Jacqueline Moudeina. On an unusually hot and dusty January day in N'Djamena, I was keen to speak to her again. I'd been calling for days, trying to get her to commit to an interview time, but she repeatedly told me she was too busy and had a headache. Finally she gave me a window just a few hours before my flight. Exhausted I jumped in the car and headed out to her house as the sun started to set hazily through the Saharan dust. She lives behind a huge gate in an unpaved street. Her lethargic guard let me in and indicated the open front door. I called out. No response. Tentatively I knocked at the door. 'Oui' came an exhausted voice. I crept into the dark living room. In one corner of the room was an astonishing Christmas tree flashing fluorescent colours that made the room look like a nightclub. Mini plastic fairy lights in the shape of jovial smiling Santas trailed across a pile of unopened presents, even though it was already mid-January. As my eyes adjusted to the darkness, I made out Jacqueline sitting on her couch, eating a huge plate of *boule* and *sauce gombo* (okra), Chad's great delicacy. She was not wearing any make-up and her short hair was untidy. She was wrapped loosely in a patterned panier and looked a little haunted. As I nervously sat down beside her, it was hard to think of a time when I'd met someone who seemed more reluctant to talk to me.

'You journalists just want the story. You just want the quote. Then you write your piece and get paid and never think about us again', she said gruffly.[20] Although I felt as though I'd actually made quite a good effort visiting Chad while six months pregnant, espe-cially when writing a book is no way to make money, it was hard to argue with her. She had only just got back from Dakar where the final bruising Appeals hearing had just ended. She'd been chased from pillar to post for days by the world's media, and she needed to let off steam.

> I'm so tired. Everyone just sees the dramatic moments in Dakar, the occasional good news. They don't have any idea that I've been battling alongside these victims for twenty-five years. I've had twenty-five years of personal sacrifices, missed family gatherings, missed meals, working for free and I'll never get that time and money back. Every day when I go to the office there are still poor victims standing outside and asking me to help with the compensation claims. I can't say no to them after all this time, but I feel like there is no end to this. I never ever thought it would take this long. When do I get my life back?

After a while she calmed down and she laughingly agreed it was a big deal making such a long trip to Chad while pregnant. We got to talking about the things she would have liked to change about the trial. She was characteristically effusive. She criticised the EAC for not being strong enough to take on the political challenge of ques-tioning the support that Habré enjoyed during his time in power: 'Habré was silent because he was covering for the US and France. We should have found more out about this. But the DDS oath was like a pact between them all, they were never going to tell anyone what really went on'. She was annoyed that the compensation issue appears to be getting kicked into the long grass, but nevertheless she worried that focusing on money risks diminishing the impact of the judicial victory: 'How many of the victims really realised this was an immense fight against impunity? That was what it was all about. And that's the problem, it's actually a fight that on this continent has no end'.

In her darkest moments, the fifteen long years from the first indictment in Senegal to the eventual opening of the EAC in Dakar, what kept her going all these years?

It was the friendships and the sense of working together on something. We did it together with the victims. It became a personal fight and I couldn't let it go. But when we got that conviction, I knew that everything had been worth it. We got our recognition. It was the proudest day of my life.

Hissene Habre 1982 1990, https://w[...]
dictator/united-states-and-chads-hi[...]

Maliveras, K. D. (2014) 'Fighting Impur[...]
the AU's Handling of the Hissene H.[...]
Comparative Law 22 (3): 420 47.

Magnien, N. (2015) 'Report on DDS Tr[...]
Definition of Command Responsibil[...]
www.peaceandjusticeinitiative.or[...]
responsibility

McAuliffe, P. (2011) 'Hybrid Tribunals [...]
Child became an Orphan', *Journ[...]
Relations 7: 1 65.

Nouwen, S. M. H. H. (2008) 'Hybrid C[...]
of International Crimes Court', *Utr[...]

Schiff, B. (2008) *Building the Internatior*[...]
University Press.

Silva, R., Klingner, J. and Weikart, S. (2[...]
under Hissène Habré: A Report b[...]
Group to Human Rights Watch a[...]
Political Repression and Crimes',[...]
chad.shtml

Stromseth, J. E. (2009) *Justice on the C*[...]
Strengthen Domestic Rule of Law in[...]
law.georgetown.edu/cgi/viewconte[...]

Whiting, A. (2009) 'In International Cr[...]
Justice Delivered', *Harvard Interna*[...]

Williams, S. (2013) 'The Extraordin[...]
Courts, An African Solution to ar[...]
Criminal Justice 11.

Woodward, B. (2005) *Veil: The Secret W*[...]
and Schuster.

É

w.hrw.org/report/2016/06/28/enabling-
sene-habre-1982-1990

y Unsuccessfully in Africa: A Critique of
re Affair', *African Journal of International*

l', *Justice Tribune*, 25 March.

y: Peace and Justice Initiative, http://
implementation-resources/command-

Ten, How International Justice's Golden
of International Law and International

rts: The Hybrid Category of a New Type
ht Law Review 2 (2): 190 214.

Criminal Court, Cambridge: Cambridge

10) 'State Coordinated Violence in Chad
Benetech's Human Rights Data Analysis
the Chadian Association of Victims of
February, http://www.hrdag.org/about/

ound: Can International Criminal Courts
ost-Conflict Societies?*, http://scholarship.
.cgi?article=1593&context=facpub

inal Prosecutions, Justice Delayed can be
nal Law Journal 50 (2).

African Chambers in the Senegalese
African Problem', *Journal of International*

of the CIA, 1981 1987, New York: Simon

INTERVIEWS

Abaifouta, Clement, Chadian Victims Association, interview in person at the trial 20 July 2015; phone interview 1 March 2017.

Abakar, Mahamat Hassan, Chadian Truth Commission former Chairman, interview N'Djamena 17 January 2017.

Ankumah, Evelyn, Director African Legal Aid, Skype interview 16 October 2017.

Bekele, Daniel, former Human Rights Watch Africa programme, interview 28 September 2017.

Brody, Reed, Human Rights Watch, Skype interview 10 March 2017; various other face-to-face interviews in Dakar.

Clark, Phil, academic, interviews London 9 January 2017, 13 April 2017.

Chadian Victims of the Crimes of Hissène Habré, via Clement Abaifouta (twenty victims), interview 17 January 2017.

Diab Nader, Redress, Skype interview 27 March 2017; phone interview March 2017.

Djinadoum, Blaise, Chadian journalist, interview Dakar 21 July 2015.

Dottridge, Mike, Amnesty International Central Africa researcher 1980s/1990s, face-to-face interview London 22 December 2016.

Fall, Mbacke, Chief Prosecutor EAC, Skype interview Dakar 24 March 2017.

Guengueng, Souleymane, interview in person at the trial 20 July 2015.

Guerling, Marguerite, Former Amnesty International Chad researcher in 1980s, Skype interview 5 January 2017.

Mahadji, Yonis, victim, interview Ndjamena 17 January 2017.

Marchand, Emmanuelle, assistant to Alain Werner for civil parties, Skype interview 15 March 2017.

Mootoo, Gaetan, former Amnesty International West Africa researcher, Skype interview 8 March 2017.

Moudeina, Jacqueline, lawyer, interview N'Djamena 18 January 2017.

Nyarko, William, Africa Centre for International Law, interview 25 September 2017.

Padare, Jean Bernard, former Chadian Minister of Justice, interview N'Djamena 17 January 2017.

Petit, Franck, EAC Outreach Consortium, Skype interview 16 February 2017.

Seelinger, Kim Thuy, Director of Sexual Violence Programme at Berkeley Law School, various Skype/email exchanges throughout 2015/16.

Survey of ordinary Chadians' viewpoints via Augustin Zuzanne, N'Djamena March 2017.

Tine, Alioune, Amnesty International West Africa director, Skype interview 8 March 2017.

Thulliez, Henri, former Human Rights Watch observer, Skype interview 5 January 2017.

Werner, Alain, lawyer for civil parties, Skype interview 25 April 2017.

NOTES

Introduction

1 Marguerite Guerling Skype interview January 2017.
2 Tim Allen 2006, p. 8.
3 Phil Clark interview January 2017.
4 Kim Thu Seelinger Skype interview April 2017.

Chapter 1

1 Burr and Collins 2008, p. 26.
2 Burr and Collins 2008, p. 33.
3 Burr and Collins 2008, p. 88.
4 http://www.chambresafricaines.org/pdf/Jugement_complet.pdf, p. 82.
5 Burr and Collins 2008, p. 107.
6 Burr and Collins 2008, p. 155.
7 Human Rights Watch 2016.
8 Human Rights Watch 2013.
9 Human Rights Watch 2013.
10 Ibid., p. 123.
11 Human Rights Watch 2013.
12 Marguerite Guerling Skype interview January 2017.
13 Human Rights Watch 2013, p. 14.
14 Burr and Collins 2008, p. 172.
15 Burr and Collins 2008, p. 229.
16 Burr and Collins 2008, p. 149.
17 http://www.lemonde.fr/afrique/article/2016/05/31/le-rapport-de-human-rights-watch-qui-pointe-la-complaisance-de-la-france_4929659_3212.html
18 Bronner 2014.
19 Emerson 1988, p. 36.
20 Woodward 2005, p. 94.
21 Human Rights Watch 2016.
22 Bronner 2014.
23 http://www.nytimes.com/1983/07/20/world/us-military-aid-to-chad.html
24 Human Rights Watch 2016.

25 Human Rights Watch 2016.
26 https://www.washingtonpost.com/archive/politics/2000/11/27/chads-torture-victims-pursue-Habré-in-court/9da03c6b-ed13-477e-9e94-7f80450ca3b8/
27 Human Rights Watch 2016.
28 http://www.lemonde.fr/afrique/article/2016/05/31/le-rapport-de-human-rights-watch-qui-pointe-la-complaisance-de-la-france_4929659_3212.html
29 Human Rights Watch 2016, p. 35.
30 Human Rights Watch 2016, p. 2.
31 http://forumchambresafricaines.org/jours-7-8-mike-dottridge-temoin-rigoureux-sur-les-crimes/
32 Mike Dottridge interview December 2016.
33 Mike Dottridge email 8 December 2016.
34 Ibid.
35 Human Rights Watch 2016.
36 Mike Dottridge interview December 2016.
37 https://archive.org/stream/countryreportson1987unit/countryreportson1987 unit_djvu.txt
38 Human Rights Watch 2016.
39 Woodward 2005, p. 158.
40 Bronner 2014.
41 Report of the Commission of Inquiry 1992, p. 64.
42 Human Rights Watch 2016.
43 http://www.lemonde.fr/afrique/article/2016/05/31/le-rapport-de-human-rights-watch-qui-pointe-la-complaisance-de-la-france_4929659_3212.html
44 Human Rights Watch 2016.
45 http://www.markhuband.com/tripoli-protests-as-us-flies-out-libyan-contras/
46 Darcourt 2001, p. 36.
47 Human Rights Watch 2013.
48 Human Rights Watch 2016.
49 Human Rights Watch 2013, p. 15.
50 Human Rights Watch 2016.
51 Bronner 2014.
52 Human Rights Watch 2016.
53 Mahamat Hassan Abakar interview January 2017.
54 Darcourt 2001, p. 10.
55 Reed Brody Skype interview March 2017.
56 Woodward 2005, p. 215.

Chapter 2

1 http://www.lemonde.fr/afrique/article/2015/09/06/le-cher-voisin-de-dakar_4747446_3212.html

2   http://ref.lamartinieregroupe.com/media/9782021189827/118982_extrait_
    Extrait_0.pdf, p. 221.
3   Report of the Commission of Inquiry 1992, p. 65.
4   http://www.lemonde.fr/afrique/article/2015/09/06/le-cher-voisin-de-dakar_
    4747446_3212.html
5   Alioune Tine Skype interview March 2017.
6   https://www.usip.org/sites/default/files/file/resources/collections/
    commissions/Chad-Report.pdf
7   Mahamat Hassan Abakar interview January 2017.
8   Report of the Commission of Inquiry 1992, p. 93.
9   Amnesty International Annual Report 1996.
10 Mahamat Hassan Abakar interview 2017.
11 Africa South of the Sahara 2016.
12 Amnesty International Annual Report 1992
13 Amnesty International Annual Report 1993.
14 Amnesty International 1996.
15 https://www.hrw.org/news/2005/01/20/chadian-feared-torturer-removed-
    un-mission-cote-divoire
16 http://tchadoscopie.over-blog.com/article-22856273.html
17 Bronner 2014.
18 https://www.hrw.org/sites/default/files/reports/chad1013frwebwcover_0.
    pdf, p. 260.
19 Clement Abaifouta phone interview March 2017.
20 https://www.hrw.org/legacy/campaigns/chile98/precedent.htm
21 Reed Brody Skype interview March 2017.
22 Bronner 2014.
23 https://www.hrw.org/legacy/campaigns/chile98/precedent.htm
24 Ibid.
25 https://www.hrw.org/news/2015/04/27/chronology-Habré-case
26 Yonis Mahadji interview January 2017.
27 Magliveras 2014, p. 427.
28 https://www.hrw.org/news/2000/10/26/chad-Hissène-Habrés-victims-
    demand-justice
29 http://foreignpolicy.com/2010/03/09/inside-a-dictators-secret-police/
30 https://www.hrw.org/news/2003/08/01/belgium-universal-jurisdiction-law-
    repealed
31 https://www.hrw.org/news/2012/03/29/Habré-case-qa-belgium-v-senegal
32 https://www.hrw.org/legacy/pub/2006/french/cat051806.pdf
33 https://www.hrw.org/news/2015/04/27/chronology-Habré-case
34 Magliveras 2014, p. 428.
35 Reed Brody interview March 2017.
36 http://www.un.org/apps/news/story.asp?NewsID=38993#.WFfYiVxrZBI

37 Clement Abaifouta phone interview March 2017.
38 http://www.bbc.com/news/world-africa-17508098
39 Reed Brody interview July 2015.
40 http://www.jurist.org/paperchase/2012/07/icj-rules-senegal-must-try-or-extradite-former-chad-dictator-Hissène-Habré.php
41 http://www.nytimes.com/2012/07/21/world/africa/senegal-to-prosecute-former-president-of-chad-Hissène-Habré.html
42 Magliveras 2014, p. 443.
43 Reed Brody Skype interview March 2017.
44 http://forumchambresafricaines.org/docs/Statute_of_the_Extraordinary_African_Chambers.pdf
45 Holvoert and de Hert 2012, p. 235.
46 Ibid.
47 McAuliffe 2011, p. 5.
48 McAuliffe 2011, p. 2.
49 Williams 2013, p. 1149.
50 Ibid., Article 3 jurisdiction.
51 https://www.hrdag.org/content/chad/State-Violence-in-Chad.pdf, p. 15.
52 http://www.peaceandjusticeinitiative.org/implementation-resources/command-responsibility
53 Phil Clark interview April 2017.
54 http://www.chambresafricaines.org/index.php/le-coin-des-medias/communiqu%C3%A9-de-presse/496-mission-parquet-general-en-belgique.html
55 http://www.chambresafricaines.org/index.php/le-coin-des-medias/communiqu%C3%A9-de-presse/495-mission-parquet-general-au-tchad.html
56 http://www.bbc.com/news/world-africa-23119658
57 https://www.theguardian.com/global-development/2013/jul/11/Hissène-Habré-chad-justice
58 Henri Thulliez Skype interview 2017.
59 Ibid.
60 http://www.smallarmssurveysudan.org/fileadmin/docs/working-papers/SAS-CAR-WP43-Chad-Sudan-Libya.pdf, p. 147.
61 https://www.hrw.org/news/2015/03/25/chad-Habré-era-agents-convicted-torture
62 Magnien 2015.
63 Ibid.
64 https://www.reuters.com/article/us-chad-habre-accomplices/chad-court-convicts-habre-era-security-officials-of-war-crimes-torture-idUSKBN0ML1UM20150325
65 Magliveras 2014, p. 445.
66 Jean-Bernard Padare interview January 2017.
67 Reed Brody Skype interview March 2017.

Chapter 3

1   https://www.youtube.com/watch?v=5oH7mBf651I
2   http://www.bbc.com/news/world-africa-33592142
3   http://www.lemonde.fr/afrique/article/2015/07/27/proces-Habré-c-est-notre-strategie-une-defense-de-refus_4700251_3212.html
4   Clement Abaifouta interview 2015; Blaise Djinadoum interview 21 July 2015.
5   Ibid.
6   Ibid.
7   http://www.bbc.com/news/world-africa-34172456
8   http://forumchambresafricaines.org/jours-7-8-mike-dottridge-temoin-rigoureux-sur-les-crimes/
9   Mike Dottridge interview December 2016.
10 https://www.youtube.com/watch?v=D5u6BL2bvxw&list=PLdiYVTzvsPW FD8s9yATKcapYT7keDWIb4&index=142
11 Mike Dottridge email 28 February 2017.
12 http://forumchambresafricaines.org/synthese-devant-les-cae-mahamat-hassan-abakar-chiffre-lhorreur-a-40-000-morts/
13 Mahamat Hassan Abakar interview January 2017.
14 http://forumchambresafricaines.org/synthese-devant-les-cae-mahamat-hassan-abakar-chiffre-lhorreur-a-40-000-morts/
15 Bronner 2014.
16 http://forumchambresafricaines.org/un-ancien-agent-de-la-dds-temoigne-je-demande-a-Habré-de-prendre-ses-responsabilites/
17 http://forumchambresafricaines.org/laccuse-Habré-interpelle-sur-les-repressions-contre-les-hadjarais/
18 https://www.hrw.org/sites/default/files/reports/chad1013frwebwcover_0.pdf, p. 332.
19 Human Rights Watch 2013.
20 https://www.hrw.org/reports/2005/chad0705/chad0705.pdf, p. 10.
21 https://www.hrw.org/report/2016/06/28/enabling-dictator/united-states-and-chads-Hissène-Habré-1982-1990
22 http://forumchambresafricaines.org/synthese-devant-les-cae-quatre-femmes-deportees-a-ouadi-doum-temoignent-dabus-sexuels/
23 http://forumchambresafricaines.org/docs/Statute_of_the_Extraordinary_African_Chambers.pdf, p. 2, Article 6.
24 http://www.refugee-rights.org/Assets/PDFs/2015/Open%20letter%20-%20 sexual%20violence.pdf
25 https://www.theguardian.com/global-development/2015/dec/22/chad-Hissène-Habré-lawyers-sexual-slavery-rape-charges-trial
26 https://www.law.berkeley.edu/wp-content/uploads/2015/04/MICUS-CURIAE-BRIEF-OF-THE-HUMAN-RIGHTS-CENTER-AT-THE-

UNIVERSITY-OF-CALIFORNIA-BERKELEY-SCHOOL-OF-LAW-AND-INTERNATIONAL-EXPERTS-ON-SEXUAL-VIOLENCE-UNDER-INTERNATIONAL-CRIMINAL-LAW-Eng.pdf, p. 2.

27 https://www.theguardian.com/global-development/2016/feb/08/Hissène-Habré-war-crimes-trial-defence-lawyers-begin-summing-up

28 http://forumchambresafricaines.org/synthese-fin-des-temoignages-au-proces-de-hissein-Habré/

29 Reed Brody interview February 2016.

30 http://forumchambresafricaines.org/un-ancien-agent-de-la-dds-temoigne-je-demande-a-Habré-de-prendre-ses-responsabilites/

31 http://www.chambresafricaines.org/pdf/Jugement_complet.pdf, p. 295.

32 http://www.usip.org/sites/default/files/file/resources/collections/commissions/Chad-Report.pdf, p. 66.

33 http://forumchambresafricaines.org/synthese-requisitoire-du-parquet-dans-le-proces-de-hissein-Habré/, plus me at the court session.

34 Reed Brody interview March 2017.

35 http://ilareporter.org.au/2016/07/the-case-of-Hissène-Habré-before-the-extraordinary-african-chambers-alexis-brassil-hedger/

36 https://www.theguardian.com/world/2016/may/30/chad-Hissène-Habré-guilty-crimes-against-humanity-senegal

37 Jacqueline Moudeina interview 2017.

38 http://www.chambresafricaines.org/pdf/Jugement_complet.pdf, p. 449.

39 Ibid., p. 501.

40 Ibid., annexe I, p. 578.

41 http://forumchambresafricaines.org/docs/Statute_of_the_Extraordinary_African_Chambers.pdf, articles 27,28.

42 https://justicehub.org/article/ex-chadian-dictator-Hissène-Habré-ordered-pay-millions-victims

43 Nader Diab Skype interview March 2017.

44 Ibid.

45 https://justicehub.org/article/ex-chadian-dictator-Hissène-Habré-ordered-pay-millions-victims

46 Nader Diab phone interview March 2017.

47 http://forumchambresafricaines.org/communique-de-presse-verdict-du-proces-en-appel-dans-laffaire-hissein-Habré-devant-les-cae/

48 Defence brief to Appeals Chamber, p. 4.

49 http://www.lesoleil.sn/component/k2/item/50400-sidiki-kaba-ministre-de-la-justice-c-est-un-proces-juste-et-equitable.html

50 https://www.theguardian.com/world/2017/apr/27/conviction-chad-Hissène-Habré-crimes-against-humanity-upheld

51 Ibid.

52 Kim Thuy Seelinger Skype interview April 2017.

53   http://www.redress.org/downloads/1704-Habré.pdf
54   Nader Diab email 4 May 2017.

Chapter 4

1   All interviews Ndjamena 16/17 January 2017.
2   Reed Brody interview March 2017.
3   Henri Thulliez Skype interview January 2017.
4   http://www.chambresafricaines.org/pdf/Jugement_complet.pdf, p. 226.
5   Ibid., p. 234.
6   http://www.rfi.fr/afrique/20150908-senegal-tchad-justice-Hissène-Habré-temoignage-ancien-presidence
7   Jacqueline Moudeina interview January 2017.
8   http://admin.gga.org/stories/editions/aif-35-balancing-justice/cross-border-justice
9   Raised during Film Africa debate, Hackney Picturehouse London 9 November 2016.
10   Reed Brody Skype interview 10 March 2017.
11   Le Monde, http://www.lemonde.fr/afrique/article/2015/07/27/proces-habre-c-est-notre-strategie-une-defense-de-refus_4700251_3212.html
12   https://www.hrw.org/news/2016/05/03/qa-case-Hissène-Habré-extraordinary-african-chambers-senegal#14
13   http://www.chambresafricaines.org/pdf/Jugement_complet.pdf p65
14   Ibid, p. 406.
15   https://www.hrw.org/news/2015/10/22/senegal-Hissène-Habré-trial-sexual-slavery-accounts
16   Nouwen 2008, p. 1.
17   Stromseth 2009, p. 89.
18   http://www.rscsl.org/Documents/slfinalreport.pdf, p. 11.
19   Ibid., p. 25.
20   https://www.opensocietyfoundations.org/sites/default/files/performance-perception-eccc-20160211.pdf, p. 85.
21   https://www.ijmonitor.org/2014/03/khmer-rouge-tribunal-urged-to-step-up-outreach/
22   https://www.ijmonitor.org/2013/08/q-a-with-international-criminal-court-registrar-herman-von-hebel-part-ii/
23   Phil Clark interview January 2017.
24   https://www.icc-cpi.int/itemsDocuments/ICC-Registry-CR.pdf, p. 157.
25   Stromseth 2009.
26   http://forumchambresafricaines.org/docs/Statute_of_the_Extraordinary_African_Chambers.pdf Article 10, p. 3.
27   Franck Petit Skype interview February 2017.

28 Ibid.
29 http://www.forumchambresafricaines.org
30 https://www.hrw.org/news/2016/05/03/qa-case-hissene-habre-extraordinary-african-chambers-senegal
31 Blaise Djimadoum interview July 2015.
32 Franck Petit Skype interview 16 February 2017.
33 https://justicehub.org/article/are-extraordinary-african-chambers-soft-Habré
34 http://www.business-anti-corruption.com/country-profiles/chad
35 Jean Bernard Padare interview January 2017.
36 Magnien 2015.
37 Phil Clark interview March 2017.
38 Mbacké Fall Skype interview March 2017.

Chapter 5

1   http://www.amnestyusa.org/news/press-releases/Hissène-Habré-verdict-is-a-landmark-decision-bringing-justice-for-tens-of-thousands-of-victims
2   http://www.reuters.com/article/us-africa-justice/chad-war-crimes-verdict-a-milestone-on-long-road-to-african-rights-court-idUSKCN0YP1PP
3   http://www.worldpoliticsreview.com/articles/18983/is-Habré-s-landmark-conviction-a-new-model-for-international-justice
4   https://www.nytimes.com/2016/02/16/opinion/the-landmark-trial-of-Hissène-Habré.html?_r=0
5   Schiff 2008, p. 3.
6   Bosco 2014, p. 76.
7   McAuliffe 2011, p. 5.
8   McAuliffe 2011, p. 6.
9   Bosco 2014, p. 23.
10 Schiff 2008, p. 48.
11 Schiff 2008, p. 32.
12 Bosco 2014, p. 185.
13 Cole 2013, p. 673.
14 Allen 2006, p. 37.
15 Bosco 2014, p. 97.
16 Allen 2006, p. 84.
17 Schiff 2008, p. 202.
18 Allen 2006, p.97.
19 Allen 2006, p. 209.
20 https://www.theguardian.com/law/2017/jan/16/trial-ex-child-soldier-dominic-ongwen-to-hear-prosecution-case-icc-uganda
21 Schiff 2008, p. 213.
22 Bosco 2014, p. 142.

23 Bosco 2014, p. 113.

24 Bosco 2014, p. 142.

25 Crilly 2010, p. 212.

26 Crilly 2010, p. 211.

27 https://www.theguardian.com/world/2010/jul/22/chad-refuses-arrest-omar-al-bashir

28 https://www.theguardian.com/world/2016/mar/16/south-african-court-rules-failure-to-detain-omar-al-bashir-was-disgraceful

29 https://www.icc-cpi.int/kenya

30 https://www.ijmonitor.org/kenya-cases-background/

31 https://www.nytimes.com/2016/06/26/magazine/international-criminal-court-moreno-ocampo-the-prosecutor-and-the-president.html?_r=1

32 http://www.bbc.com/news/world-africa-23359940

33 https://www.hrw.org/news/2016/04/05/icc-kenya-deputy-presidents-case-ends

34 https://www.nytimes.com/2016/06/26/magazine/international-criminal-court-moreno-ocampo-the-prosecutor-and-the-president.html?_r=1

35 http://www.bbc.com/news/world-africa-29083115

36 https://www.nytimes.com/2016/06/26/magazine/international-criminal-court-moreno-ocampo-the-prosecutor-and-the-president.html?_r=1

37 https://twitter.com/UKenyatta/status/808263974231928832

38 http://www.bbc.com/news/world-africa-35965760

39 https://www.washingtonpost.com/news/monkey-cage/wp/2016/02/03/who-is-laurent-gbagbo-and-why-is-he-on-trial-at-the-icc/?utm_term=.9aeb87824be4

40 https://www.icc-cpi.int/pages/item.aspx?name=pr1242

41 https://justiceinconflict.org/2016/08/25/the-al-mahdi-case-is-a-break-through-for-the-international-criminal-court/

42 https://www.hrw.org/news/2017/02/01/aus-icc-withdrawal-strategy-less-meets-eye

43 William Nyarko interview 2017.

44 http://criticallegalthinking.com/2016/10/30/africa-in-the-dock-icc-bias/

45 Ibid.

46 https://justiceinconflict.org/2012/02/22/is-the-icc-racist/

47 https://justiceinconflict.org/2016/10/26/some-thoughts-on-south-africas-withdrawal-from-the-international-criminal-court/

48 Cole 2013, p. 687.

49 Phil Clark interview March 2017.

50 Crilly 2010, p. 223.

51 Crilly 2010, p. 224.

52 Allen 2006, p. 24.

53 http://www.independent.co.uk/news/world/africa/gambia-international-criminal-court-hague-yahya-jammeh-south-africa-burundi-a7380516.html
54 https://www.theguardian.com/law/2017/jan/31/african-leaders-plan-mass-withdrawal-from-international-criminal-court
55 Phil Clark interview January 2017.
56 Whiting 2009, p. 327.
57 https://www.theguardian.com/world/2016/dec/07/the-gambias-new-rulers-vow-to-prosecute-outgoing-president
58 Reed Brody phone interview 10 March 2017.
59 http://www.justiceinfo.net/en/justice-reconciliation/34449-lawyer-who-felled-habr%C3%A9-to-pursue-gambian-yahya-jammeh.html
60 http://www.reuters.com/article/us-gambia-justice-victims/victims-of-chads-former-ruler-inspire-gambians-seeking-jammeh-justice-idUSKB
     N17Z1O0
61 https://www.nytimes.com/2016/02/16/opinion/the-landmark-trial-of-Hissène-Habré.html?_r=0
62 Williams 2013, p. 1140.
63 Evelyn Ankumah interview October 2017.
64 http://www.bbc.co.uk/news/world-africa-34477883
65 https://www.dailymaverick.co.za/article/2015-09-08-analysis-africa-might-not-see-the-likes-of-habr-and-ntaganda-in-court-again-this-decade/#.
     WMf_039rZBI
66 Williams 2013, p. 1152 n. 67.
67 Williams 2013.

Conclusion

1   Jacqueline Moudeina interview 2017.
2   My survey carried out by Augustin Zuzanne.
3   Gaetan Mootoo Skype interview March 2017.
4   Emmanuelle Marchand Skype interview March 2017.
5   Williams 2013, p. 1139.
6   Ibid.
7   https://www.iol.co.za/news/africa/Habré-trial-to-show-off-african-justice-1871192
8   Kim Thuy Seelinger Skype interview April 2017.
9   http://www.sen360.fr/actualite/la-justice-africaine-fete-la-victoire-501301.html
10 Evelyn Ankumah Skype interview October 2017.
11 Phil Clark interview January 2017.
12 https://www.hrw.org/news/2017/02/21/step-toward-justice-central-african-republic

13 https://justiceinconflict.org/2017/06/07/the-road-ahead-building-momen-tum-for-justice-in-the-central-african-republic%e2%80%a8/

14 Kersten Labuda part one.

15 Mbacké Fall Skype interview March 2017.

16 https://thehaguetrials.co.ke/nine-things-about-african-court-justice-and-human-rights/article

17 AU Reuters chad Habré iyanda.

18 Reed Brody Skype interview March 2017.

19 Mbacké Fall Skype interview March 2017.

20 Jacqueline Moudeina interview January 2017.

INDEX

Women and the War on Boko Haram: Wives, Weapons, Witnesses
BY HILARY MATFESS

'An original, innovative, and much-needed addition to the growing literatures on both women and conflict in Africa and the Boko Haram insurgency.'

Brandon Kendhammer, Ohio University

'The author's intensive fieldwork reveals previously unseen layers of complexity. Matfess is right to conclude the fate of Nigeria is tied to the fate of its women, and her book is an important contribution to that discussion.'

Valerie Hudson, Texas A&M University

Congo's Violent Peace: Conflict and Struggle Since the Great African War
BY KRIS BERWOUTS

'Essential reading for all those who want to understand the current situation. *Congo's Violent Peace* has all the makings of a classic.'

Séverine Autesserre, author of *The Trouble with the Congo and Peaceland*

'Few people have a better grasp of the key players than Kris Berwouts. From diplomat parties to refugee camps, from warlords to the presidential entourage, this book is essential reading for anyone truly interested in the DRC.'

David Van Reybrouck, author of *Congo: The Epic History of a People*

Africa: Why Economists Get It Wrong
BY MORTEN JERVEN

'A highly readable and absolutely devastating critique of an increasingly extensive and influential body of work by economists seeking to explain "what's wrong with Africa".'

James Ferguson, Stanford University

'Morten Jerven provides a valuable reminder of the need not just to cite statistics but to question them.'

Financial Times